The Passion for Romance

The writers included here, who come from all sides of the political spectrum, celebrate the romance novel as a truly feminist expression of the heroine's power over herself, her world, and her hero. Although critics might scoff at the literary value of romantic novels, readers and writers alike understand the messages, morals, and values inherent in every romance. This anthology goes a long way toward explaining and encouraging the nature and appeal of the most popular kind of novel being written today.

Dangerous
MEN &
Adventurous
WOMEN

*Romance Writers on the
Appeal of the Romance*

EDITED BY
Jayne Ann Krentz

HarperPaperbacks
A Division of HarperCollinsPublishers

HarperPaperbacks *A Division of* HarperCollins*Publishers*
10 East 53rd Street, New York, N.Y. 10022

A trade paperback edition of this book was published in 1992 by University of Pennsylvania Press as part of the New Cultural Studies.

First HarperPaperbacks printing: June 1996

Printed in the United States of America

HarperPaperbacks, HarperMonogram, and colophon are trademarks of HarperCollins*Publishers*

10   9   8   7   6   5   4   3   2   1

*For Patricia Reynolds Smith,
an editor with vision.
Her love of the romance novel
together with her dedication to
scholarly publishing transformed
this book from dream to reality.*

Contents

Acknowledgments

I wish to begin these acknowledgments with loving thanks to my husband, Frank, whose love and support have never wavered.

This book was born out of a host of conversations that took place over the years among members of the romance writing community. Many of the women involved in these discussions have essays in this volume, but I wish also to acknowledge the benefit of insights I have garnered from other friends in the sisterhood including Linda Lael Miller, Debbie Macomber, Margaret Chittenden, and Katherine Stone.

In addition, I want to thank Janice Radway and Kay Mussell, whose distinguished work on the romance has opened doors, for their generous encouragement and support of this project.

A very special thanks goes to my agent Steven Axelrod for his professional support and encouragement. His advice has been invaluable over the years.

All of us who write romance are indebted to our spiritual foremothers, the countless generations of storytelling women who preceded us. We are part of an unbroken female line dedicated to passing on an ancient tradition of literature written by women for women.

Dangerous
MEN&
Adventurous
WOMEN

*Romance Writers on the
Appeal of the Romance*

JAYNE ANN KRENTZ

Introduction

Few people realize how much courage it takes for a woman to open a romance novel on an airplane. She knows what everyone around her will think about both her and her choice of reading material. When it comes to romance novels, society has always felt free to sit in judgment not only on the literature but on the reader herself.

The verdict is always the same. Society does not approve of the reading of romance novels. It labels the books as trash and the readers as unintelligent, uneducated, unsophisticated, or neurotic.

The fact that so many women persist in reading and enjoying romance novels in the face of generations of relentless hostility says something profound not only about women's courage but about the appeal of the books.

No one who reads or writes romance expects to be able to teach critics to appreciate the novels. As any romance reader or writer will tell you, a reader either enjoys the novels or she does not. If she does, no further explanations of the appeal of the books are necessary.

The same is true of the other genres. A reader who does not intuitively respond to horror or science fiction novels cannot be persuaded by logic or argument to enjoy either genre. The difference is that the person who does not like to read horror or science fiction is unlikely to criticize the genres or chastise and condemn the readers who do love them but simply shrugs and accepts the fact that the stories hold no personal appeal.

The most popular genres of fiction are based on fantasies, creations of the imagination which are not intended to conform to real life. Robert Ludlum plots many of his books around bizarre conspiracies. His heroes escape from situations in which, in real life, escape would be extremely unlikely. Stephen King presents us with pets that come back from the dead and little girls who can use mental powers to send buildings up in flames. Anne McCaffrey creates flying dragons. Robert Parker and Dick Francis invent heroes who work outside the normal structure of the law enforcement system to solve murders on their own.

Most people understand and accept the way in which fantasy works when they sit down to read Ludlum, King, McCaffrey or the others. Furthermore everyone understands that the readers know the difference between real life and fantasy and that they do not expect one to imitate the other. But, for some reason, when it comes to romance novels critics worry about whether the women who read them can tell the difference between what is real and what is not.

Of course the readers can tell the difference. They do not expect the imaginative creations of romance to conform to real life any more than they expect the fantasies of any other genre to conform to the real world. Like all the other genres, romance is based on fantasies and readers know it. Readers and writers alike get disgusted with critics who express concern that they may not be able to step back out of the fantasy. They do not appreciate being treated as if they were children who don't know where one stops and the other begins.

The contributors to this collection of essays did not set out to provide a set of closely reasoned arguments in defense of the romance novel. What the writers in this volume have tried to do is explain to those who do not understand the appeal of the books that this appeal is as complex as it is powerful. They have tried to show that the criteria used to evaluate "literary" fiction are inadequate either to identify what readers find so satisfying about romance or to distinguish, as readers clearly do, between good romance and bad.

The writers included in this collection represent a cross section of the genre. Some of them write the short, contemporary series romances such as those published by Harlequin and Silhouette. Others write single-title releases, historical and contemporary. They are all proven successes as romance novelists. Each has several published books to her credit. Individual print-runs range from over a hundred thousand to over a million. Most of the writers in this volume have been given awards by their peers, fans, and booksellers. Most have appeared on the Waldenbooks, Barnes and Noble, and B. Dalton bestseller lists. Several appear routinely on the *New York Times* and *Washington Post* bestseller lists.

In addition to representing a wide spectrum of the romance market, the writers also represent a cross section of the nation. They hail from both coasts, the South, and the Midwest. There are also two contributors from New Zealand.

All the contributors, like the vast majority of romance readers, are women. Most are involved in long term marriages; many have children. Before pursuing their writing careers they were employed in a variety of fields including business, law, journalism, engineering, and education. Their experiences have made them well aware of such things as glass ceilings and old boy networks. Most consider themselves feminists, although they recognize that their definition of feminism may not coincide with that of all feminists.

It is interesting to note that many of the contributors discovered romance novels in college or shortly after entering the work force, at a time when they were becoming fully aware of the battles they would face as women for the rest of their lives. It is also interesting to note that none of them saw any conflict between their choice of fiction and the real world in which they lived. They did not feel threatened by the romance novels they were reading. They did not consider them politically incorrect. They feel the same way about the romance novels they create today.

With few exceptions, the women who write romance were romance readers first. They had already discovered that they enjoyed the novels before they tried to write them. Most writers in the romance genre are quick to tell you that you can't write romance successfully if you don't love to read it. It is a genre that requires absolute sincerity. Writers who "drop into" the field with the intention of churning out a few quick books in order to make some fast money rarely last long, if they manage to get published at all. If they are successful in selling a manuscript or two, the resulting books are never the ones that prove most popular with the readers.

One of the reasons it is extremely difficult to write in the genre unless you do love it is that, as Seidel notes in her essay, a writer is more or less doomed to write certain kinds of books. In romance the success of an individual author is not based on how well she writes by conventional standards, but on how compellingly she can create her fantasy and on how many readers discover they can step into it with her for a couple of hours. This is equally true for the writers in other genres. Successful authors become successful not because of their conventional writing skills but because of how accessible they make their fantasies.

Romance writers are very much in touch with their readers, partly because they are readers themselves, but also because in this genre readers tend to communicate with writers. Readers write fan letters and they meet with the writers at conferences. Of course they also make known their preferences every time they make a purchase in a bookstore. Nevertheless, nearly every successful romance writer will tell you that she does not, indeed could not, write for the readers. Romance writers, like all writers, must recreate their own vividly imagined fantasies first and then hope and pray that there will be a large number of readers who will also enjoy that particular fantasy. That is the basic reason why there is no "formula"[1] for romance writing. The books that are constructed "by the numbers" never work well in romance, just as they don't work in other genres. They lack the subtext that makes a romance novel come alive.

The essays in this volume are as diverse as the writers who contributed them. They represent a variety of viewpoints as well as the individual voices and styles the authors bring to their novels. And there is great variety within the romance genre. It is a serious mistake to assume that all the books are alike.

The notion that the romance genre contains only one

single, monolithic story that is cranked out over and over again should be dispelled after an examination of this volume. Anyone who knows anything at all about the creative process will understand that no two of the writers in this book could possibly fashion exactly the same story, even if they deliberately tried to do so.

Each essay in this volume reflects the unique view of the writer who wrote it. The writers developed their theories on the appeal of the novel independently and reached their own conclusions. But as the essays began arriving on the editor's desk, several unifying themes emerged.

First and foremost among these themes is an exasperated declaration that the romance novel is based on fantasies and that the readers are no more confused about this fact, nor any more likely to use their reading as a substitute for action in the real world, than readers of Ludlum, Parker, Francis, and McCaffrey.

The second, equally strong theme that emerges from the essays is that of female empowerment. Readers understand that the books celebrate female power. In the romance novel, as Phillips, Clair, and several others point out, the woman always wins. With courage, intelligence, and gentleness she brings the most dangerous creature on earth, the human male, to his knees. More than that, she forces him to acknowledge her power as a woman.

A third theme, one related to empowerment, is that of the inherently subversive nature of the romance novel. Romance novels invert the power structure of a patriarchal society because they show women exerting enormous power over men. The books also defy the masculine conventions of other forms of literature because they portray women as heroes. As Cameron and others explain, the romance novel is the only genre in which readers can routinely expect to encounter heroines who are imbued with the qualities normally reserved for the heroes in other genres: honor, courage, and determination. As Williamson notes, the hero falls in love with the heroine because he sees something of himself in her—he sees the *hero* in her. It works the other way, as well. The heroine will not accept the hero completely until she has seen some evidence of her own gentleness and compassion in him. This business of hero and heroine reflecting each other's strongest and most admirable traits is an important element in the romance novel.

The subversive nature of the books is fundamental and inescapable. Romances are, after all, stories that have been told to women by women for generations. The language of the books, so often ridiculed by critics, is essential to the novels because it is a coded language. As the Barlow and Krentz essay notes, the novels are full of allusions and resonances that are unrecognizable to outsiders.

A fourth theme in the essays is that of the integration of male and female. Some writers, such as Barlow and Kinsale, believe that this integration has nothing to do with real men at all. They feel that it is an integration, exploration, and celebration of the masculine elements every woman has deep within herself. Other writers see this integration as an event which occurs within the hero and which is brought about by the power of the heroine. In effect, these writers say, the heroine of a romance novel civilizes the hero by teaching him to combine his warrior qualities with the protective, nurturing aspects of his nature.

It should be understood that romance novels are not tales of women turning men into women. Nor are they female revenge fantasies, as some critics have suggested. They are not castration fantasies. It is true that the heroes in the books undergo a significant change in the course of the story, often being tamed or gentled or taught to love, but they do not lose any of their masculine strength in the process.

The stories make it clear that women value the warrior qualities in men as well as their protective, nurturing qualities. The trick is to teach the hero to integrate and control the two warring halves of himself so that he can function as a reliable mate and as a father. The journey of the novel, many writers say, is the civilization of the male.

The fifth theme easily identified in the essays is a belief that romance novels celebrate life. There is a deep-rooted optimism inherent in the romance novel that crosses cultural and political boundaries. The books, as Linz documents, are as successful among women readers in Japan, Eastern Europe, and Scandinavia as they are in North America. Margaret Chittenden, author of several romance novels published by Harlequin Enterprises, tells of meeting two hundred and fifty Japanese women in Tokyo a few years ago. They were all regular readers of the romances published by Ms. Chittenden's publisher. Many of the women talked to her about their enjoyment of the books. Harlequin had changed the face of romance writing in Japan, they said. Historically, they explained, love stories in their country ended in tragedy. "Everybody dies," one woman murmured. To demonstrate to Ms. Chittenden how much they appreciated the difference Harlequin had made, one woman who could not speak much English came up to her and took her by the hand. "Happy ever after, yes?" she said.

The celebration of life is expressed also in the frequency with which happy endings include the birth of a child. Babies are always treated as a cause for joy in romance, whether a writer has chosen to have children or not, whether she is in favor of abortion rights or not.

The fantasies in the books have nothing to do with a woman's politics. Even the most casual survey of the readers will reveal fundamentalists, atheists, conservatives, moderates, and liberals among them. But they all respond to romance tales that celebrate the male-female bond that will bring forth new life.

Another theme that is present in the essays has to do with reader identification. One of the first things that must be understood about romance novels is that reader identification with the characters is far more complex than critics have realized. Sometimes the reader identifies with the heroine; sometimes, as Kinsale points out in her essay, the heroine functions simply as a place-holder; and sometimes the reader identifies with the hero. The latter should not come as a surprise. Writers freely explain that when they write the novels they identify with their heroes at least as much as they do with their heroines. It is certainly true that both reader and writer slip easily in and out of the skins of the two main characters as the romance progresses.

There are also occasions in the books when the reader identifies with both hero and heroine simultaneously. This simultaneous identification is very common during love scenes. Seductions in well-written romance novels are especially powerful because the reader experiences them as both seducer and seduced. Such a phenomenon is difficult to illustrate using the standard language of literary analysis, but it is an extremely compelling form of writing.

Duality is central to another theme that emerges from the essays in this volume. Some writers, myself included, believe that a sense of danger, of risk, is created in the books by the fact that the hero plays two roles: he is both hero and villain. The challenge the heroine faces is unique to romance fiction. She must find a way to conquer the villain without destroying the hero. Such a task is far more complex than that faced by the protagonists of westerns and mysteries.

For those who understand the encoded information in the stories, the books preserve elements of ancient myths and legends that are particularly important to women. They celebrate female power, intuition, and a female worldview that affirms life and expresses hope for the future.

Critics and readers who fail to comprehend the complexity and subtlety of the genre frequently dismiss the books as poorly written or unimaginative, when the simple truth is that they just don't understand the encoded information in the text. Even the essays in this volume are, to some extent, locked in code. The problem was inevitable due to the inherent difficulty of explaining any type of fantasy experience to those who do not grasp it intuitively. Thoughtful readers of the essays will have to abandon some of the conventional critical assumptions in favor of other perspectives if they wish to comprehend much of what is said here about the nature of the appeal of the romance novel.

A brief biography of each author appears at the end of her first contribution to this volume.

NOTE

1. I am using the term "formula" in the sense in which it is used routinely in the media and in the publishing world.

JAYNE ANN KRENTZ (AMANDA QUICK, JAYNE CASTLE, STEPHANIE JAMES)

Under a variety of pseudonyms Jayne Ann Krentz has written and published more than fifty series romances for several publishers including Harlequin, Silhouette, and Dell. Many of these series romances have appeared on the Waldenbooks Romance bestseller list, including *The Private Eye*, which reached the number one position on the list.

Currently she writes contemporary romances for Pocket Books under her own name and historical romances for Bantam under the pen name Amanda Quick. Her books appear consistently on the Waldenbooks and B. Dalton bestseller lists. Several of her contemporary and historical titles, including *Scandal, Rendezvous,* and *Sweet Fortune,* appeared on the *New York Times* list. Two of her recent titles, *Scandal* and *Ravished,* were featured as alternate selections in the Doubleday Bookclub.

Ms. Krentz has a degree in history from the University of California at Santa Cruz and a master's degree in library science. Before pursuing her writing career she worked in academic and corporate libraries.

CATHIE LINZ

Setting the Stage

Facts and Figures

According to a variety of sources, romances account for a staggering 35 to 40 percent of all mass market paperback sales. The world's largest publisher of romances, Harlequin Enterprises, has reported annual sales of over 190 million books worldwide. These books are translated into over twenty languages, including Japanese, Greek, and Swedish. They are published in over 100 international markets: from North and South America, to the Far East, to Western Europe and—starting in the summer of 1990—Eastern Europe as well, with the distribution of the books in Hungary. Further expansion into Eastern Europe is planned.[1]

All of this suggests that the underlying appeal of romance novels is universal in nature, crossing cultural and political boundaries. Harlequin has opened the door and proved that the readership is there. The market seems to be an expanding one, a global community of romance readers.

Romance novels can be broken down into two broad categories: historical romances, which utilize a wide variety of historical backdrops, and contemporary romances. The distinction is important because the temporal settings have a strong influence on plot lines and the type of fantasy that is found in the books.

These two basic categories are then broken down into more specific subcategories. For example, Regency romances, set against the backdrop of Regency England, are a sub-genre of historical romances. Medieval romances are another popular sub-genre of historical romances. Series romances such as those published by Harlequin/Silhouette are a sub-genre of contemporary romances.

Romance novels run the gamut in style from the gentle and humorous to the intense and dramatic. They also vary greatly in levels of sensuality and in the amount of realistic elements incorporated in the plot lines. The tone of the fantasy in the books ranges across the spectrum from light to dark.

Therefore, saying all romances are the same is like saying all buildings are the same. To someone with an untrained eye, this may appear to be true, but an architect can tell the difference between a Louis Sullivan design and a Mies van der Rohe. So, too, can romance readers and writers tell the differences among the many types of romances available in the marketplace today.

Readers have strong preferences not only for specific sub-genres but also for specific authors. Based on the number of used bookstores that routinely fill highly specific requests from romance readers around the globe, one can assume this selective approach to reading in the genre is a worldwide phenomenon.

With the increasing presence of American writers on the scene in the past decade, the marketplace has opened up to all kinds of romance novel hybrids: time-travel love stories, science fiction/fantasy romances, romantic suspense, western romances. It should be noted that romance writers have expanded the field without abandoning the genre's roots. The basic expectations of the readers are still being fulfilled.

Demographic information on romance readers is hard to come by, as it would be for any group of readers. Harlequin Enterprises has done market research[2] on its North American readers and compiled the following statistical information:

Approximately 70 percent of the readers are women under 49 years of age. 45 percent of them have attended college. The number of readers currently involved in a relationship with a man is 79 percent. Two-thirds own their own home. Over half, 51 percent of them, work outside the home. 68 percent of romance readers read a newspaper every or nearly every day, a figure that is higher than the national average. 71 percent purchase romance novels at least once a month.

Romance readers are linked by their interest in the genre. They love to talk to each other about their favorite romance titles and authors. They exchange books and opinions and make recommendations wherever they meet—at bookstores and conferences and at the office.

Readers also use their computers and their modems to access nationwide networking systems so that they can communicate about the books with sister readers across the country. One such commercial networking system has so many members and so much activity that it presently has over a dozen subheadings under the topic of romance fiction. Members of the system go online regularly to "talk books" via computer, sharing their excitement in the wonderful variety of books available to them in the romance genre.

In the final analysis the numbers cited in this essay speak for themselves, establishing the fact that the appeal of romance is enormous and cross-cultural. The essays that follow will attempt to explain the diverse and complex nature of that appeal.

NOTES

1. Reader market data courtesy of Harlequin Enterprises Ltd., Toronto, Ontario, Canada.
2. Ibid.

CATHIE LINZ

Cathie Linz has been a full-time writer for over a decade. She has published more than twenty series romances for Dell and Silhouette. Several of her books have appeared on the Waldenbooks Romance bestseller list, including *Wildfire* which reached the number two position. *Pride and Joy* appeared on the Waldenbooks mass market bestseller list. *Adam's Way,* a Silhouette Desire, was a bestseller in Italy when it was translated and published there. *Flirting with Trouble* is the title of one of her most recent releases.

Ms. Linz is a frequent lecturer and has given numerous workshops at various writers' conferences across the country and at libraries in the Chicago area. Before pursuing her writing career full time, she was Head of Acquisitions at Northern Illinois University Law Library.

LINDA BARLOW & JAYNE ANN KRENTZ

Beneath the Surface

The Hidden Codes of Romance

Townsfolk called him devil. For dark and enigmatic Julian, Earl of Ravenwood, was a man with a legendary temper and a first wife whose mysterious death would not be forgotten. Some said the beautiful Lady Ravenwood had drowned herself in the black, murky waters of Ravenwood Pond. Others whispered of foul play and the devil's wrath.

Now country-bred Sophy Dorring is about to become Ravenwood's new bride. Drawn to his masculine strength and the glitter of desire that burned in his emerald eyes, the tawny-haired lass had her own reasons for agreeing to a marriage of convenience . . . Sophy Dorring intended to teach the devil to love.

Back cover copy for *Seduction,* by Jayne Ann Krentz writing as Amanda Quick, Bantam, 1990.

It is difficult to explain the appeal of romance novels to people who don't read them. Outsiders tend to be unable to interpret the conventional language of the genre or to recognize in that language the symbols, images, and allusions that are the fundamental stuff of romance. Moreover, romance writers are consistently attacked for their use of this language by critics who fail to fathom its complexities. In a sense, romance writers are writing in a code clearly understood by readers but opaque to others.

The author of a romance novel and her audience enter into a pact with one another. The reader trusts the writer to create and recreate for her a vision of a fictional world that is free of moral ambiguity, a larger-than-life domain in which such ideals as courage, justice, honor, loyalty, and love are challenged and upheld. It is an active, dynamic realm of conflict and resolution, evil and goodness, darkness and light, heroes and heroines, and it is a familiar world in which the roads are well-traveled and the rules are clear. The romance writer gives form and substance to this vision by locking it in language, and the romance reader yields herself to this alternative world in the act of reading, allowing the narrative to engage her mind and her emotions and to provide her with a certain intensity of experience. She knows that certain expectations will be met and that certain conventions will not be violated.

How does the romance writer construct this fictional universe? By means of the figurative language she chooses to employ—rich, evocative diction that is heavy-laden with familiar symbols, images, metaphors, paradoxes, and allusions to the great mythical traditions that reach from ancient Greece to Celtic Britain to the American West. Through this language she creates the plots, characters, and settings that evoke the vision and transport the reader into the landscape of romance.

Because the figurative language, allusions, and plot elements of the best-loved stories are so familiar and accessible, romance writers are often criticized for the lack of originality of our plots (which are regarded as contrived and formulaic) and the excessive lushness or lack of subtlety of our language. In other words, we are condemned for making use of the very codes that are most vital to our genre.

But these codes, familiar though they may be, are extremely powerful. Contained within them is a collection of subtle feminine voices, part myth, part fantasy, part reality, messages that have been passed down from one generation of women to the next. The voices arise from deep within our collective feminine psyche and consciousness, and we suspect that most women have access to them, however strongly they have been defended against or denied.

What are these messages? They include the celebration of feminine wisdom and power. Celebration of female ability to share, empathize, and communicate on the deepest levels. Celebration of the integration of male and female, both within the psyche and in society. Celebration of the reconciling power of love to heal, to renew, to affirm, and to create new life. And finally, celebration of the feminine ability to do battle on the most mythical planes of existence where emotions rise to epic levels, and to temper and transform all this energy in such a way that it is brought down to human levels by the marriage at the end of the book.

Romance novels are often criticized for certain plot elements that occur over and over in the genre—spirited young women forced into marriage with mysterious earls and heroes with dark and dangerous pasts who are bent upon vengeance rather than love. It is possible to write a romance that does not utilize these elements; indeed, it's done all the time. But the books that hit the bestseller lists are invariably those with plots that place an innocent young woman at risk with a powerful, enigmatic male. Her future happiness and *his* depend upon her ability to teach him how to love.

Writers in the genre know that the plot elements that lend themselves to such clashes are those which force the hero and heroine into a highly charged emotional situation which neither can escape without sacrificing his or her agenda: forced marriage, vengeance, kidnapping, and so forth. Such situations effectively ensure intimacy while establishing clear battle lines. They produce conflicts with stakes that are particularly important to women. They promise the possibility of a victory that romance readers find deeply satisfying: a victory that is an affirmation of life, a victory that fuses male and female.

The plot devices in romance novels are based on paradoxes, opposites, and the threat of danger. The more strongly emphasized the contrasts between hero and heroine are, the more the confrontations between the two take on a sense of the heroic. In many cases the heroine must do battle with a hero whose mythical resonance is that of the devil himself. She is light, he is darkness; she is hope, he is despair. The love that develops between them is the mediating, reconciling force.

These heroic quests are often carried out against a lush setting which subtly deepens the sense of danger by presenting yet another contrast. Dark menace can walk through a dazzling ballroom. The devil can pass in high society.

Stories that utilize these elements have always been wildly popular. After being used and reused for centuries, certain plot devices have become associated with an elaborate set of emotional and intellectual responses in the minds of both romance writers and romance readers. When she sits down to pen a novel, the romance writer takes this web of responses for granted. She knows the conventions, she understands the layers of meaning that certain words, phrases, and plot elements have accumulated through the years, and she knows how these meanings have been shaped and refined for romance. She can be confident that her readers also understand these subtleties. The worldwide popularity of romance novels is testimony to the way the familiar codes are universally recognized by women as cues for their deepest thoughts, dreams, and fantasies.

Most of the emotional and intellectual responses generated by romance plot devices are rendered complex by their paradoxical nature: marriages that are simultaneously real and false (the marriage of convenience); heroes who also function as villains; victories that are acts of surrender; seductions in which one is both seducer and seduced; acts of vengeance that conflict with acts of love. Such contradictory elements must be integrated in a happy ending for a romance novel to be deemed successful.

It is the promise of integration and reconciliation which captures the reader's imagination. She is reminded of this tacit contract between herself and the author every time she picks up a book, reads the back cover copy, and registers such code phrases as "a lust for vengeance," "a hunter stalking his prey," "marriage of convenience," "teach the devil to love." Drawing on her own emotional and intellectual background, both inside and outside the romance genre, she responds to these code phrases with lively interest and anticipation as she looks forward to the pleasurable reading experience the novel promises.

The concept of being forced to marry the devil, for instance, resonates with centuries of history, myth, and legend. Both reader and writer understand the allusions. They have knowledge on the subject of devils and demons that is wide ranging, gleaned from philosophy, theology, psychology, and literature, knowledge that encompasses many conflicting facts and cultural traditions. Both reader and writer also have a vast acquaintance with the devil-heroes who appear in romance novels, since there is a time-honored tradition of heroines sent on quests to encounter and transform these masculine creatures of darkness.

When the romance reader picks up a book that describes a marriage of convenience to such a devil-hero, she understands she is being promised a tale that will deliver a strong sense of emotional risk and at the same time resolve paradoxes and integrate opposites. The happy ending will be especially satisfying because it will have been preceded by several exciting clashes between the heroine and her beloved adversary.

To make such clashes work, the hero must be a worthy and suitably dangerous opponent, a larger-than-life male imbued with great power and a mysterious past. He will not run from the coming battle. Recognizing the allusions that testify to his mythic nature, the reader mentally girds herself for the fray when she reads the code words—phrases such as "townsfolk called him devil" on the back of the book. She glories in the expectation of the complex warfare she—in her imaginative identification with the characters—will soon wage. If the romance is well done, she will, as Kinsale and Barlow indicate in their essays elsewhere in this volume, find herself plunged into a combat in which she will fight on both sides. The romance novel will be a chess game in which the reader simultaneously plays the white and the black, a medieval joust in which she rides both horses into the lists.

Such fantasies are exquisitely subtle and require that the reader be an active participant. She will enjoy the combat, relish the danger, and, perhaps most intriguing, exercise the full range of her options. This, by the way, is one of the true joys of romance fantasies. The reader knows that in the conflict between hero and heroine the heroine will never have to pull her punches. She won't have to worry—as many modern women do in their everyday lives—about being too assertive, too aggressive, too verbally direct because this hero is as strong as she is. He is a worthy opponent, a mythic beast who is her heroic complement. He has been variously described as a devil, a demon, a tiger, a hawk, a pirate, a bandit, a potentate, a hunter, a warrior. He is definitely *not* the boy next door.

Indeed, he's a man in every sense of the word, and for most women the word *man* reverberates with thousands of years of connotative meanings which touch upon everything from sexual prowess, to the capacity for honor and loyalty, to the ability to protect and defend the family unit. He is no weakling who will run away or turn to another woman when the conflict between himself and the heroine flares. Instead, he will be forced in the course of the plot to prove his commitment to the relationship, and, unlike many men in the real world, he will pass this test magnificently.

Should the book fail to deliver on its implied promise, should the writer be unable to create the fantasy satisfactorily, make it accessible, and achieve the integration of opposites that results in a happy ending, the reader will consider herself cheated. The happy ending in a romance novel is far more significant than it might appear to those who do not understand the codes. It requires that the final union of male and female be a fusing of contrasting elements: heroes who are gentled by love yet who lose none of their warrior qualities in the process and heroines who conquer devils without sacrificing their femininity. It requires a quintessentially female kind of victory, one in which neither side loses, one which produces a whole that is stronger than either of its parts. It requires that the hero acknowledge the heroine's heroic qualities in both masculine and feminine terms. He must recognize and admire her sense of honor, courage, and determination as well as her traditionally female qualities of gentleness and compassion. And it requires a sexual bonding that transcends the physical, a bond that reader and writer know can never be broken.

Thus, as the romance novel ends, the contrasting elements in the plot are entirely fused and reconciled. Male and female are integrated. The heroine's quest is won. She has succeeded in shining light into the darkness surrounding the hero. She has taught the devil to love.

Nothing about the romance genre is more reviled by literary critics and, indeed, by the public at large, than the conventional diction of romance. Descriptive passages are regularly culled from romance novels and read aloud with great glee and mockery by everybody from college professors to talk show hosts. You would think that we romance novelists—who, like anyone else, cringe at the thought of being made the object of ridicule on national TV—would have the wit to clean up our act. After all, we are talented professionals. We're quite capable of choosing other, more subtle, less effusive forms of narrative and discourse. Yet we persist in penning sentences like "Caught up in the tender savagery of love . . . she saw him, felt him, *knew* him in a manner that, for an instant, transcended the physical. It was as if their souls yearned toward each other, and in a flash of glory, merged and became one" (Barlow, *Fires of Destiny*).

Why? Are we woefully derivative and unoriginal? Do our editors force us to write this way? Do we all have access to some sort of romance writers' phrase book to which we constantly refer? Are we incapable of expressing ourselves in any other manner?

The answer, of course, is none of the above. We write this way because we know that this is the language which best serves our purposes as romance authors. This is the language that, for romance novels, *works*. Why? Because the language of romance most effectively carries and reinforces the essential messages that we, consciously or unconsciously, are endeavoring to convey.

In our genre (and in others, we believe), stock phrases and literary figures are regularly used to evoke emotion. This is not well understood by critics of these genres. Romance readers have a keyed-in response to certain words and phrases (the sardonic lift of the eyebrows, the thundering of the heart, the penetrating glance, the low murmur or sigh). Because of their past reading experiences, readers associate certain emotions—anger, fear, passion, sorrow—with such language and expect to feel the same responses each time they come upon such phrases. This experience can be quite intense, yet, at the same time, the codes that evoke the dramatic illusion also maintain it *as* illusion (not delusion—romance readers do not confuse fantasy with reality). Encountering the familiar language, the reader responds emotionally to the characters, settings, and events in the *fictional* world of romance. And although what she feels is her own internal experience, it is something that can be shared with millions of other women around the world, so the commonality of the experience is appealing, too.

But the reader's pleasure is not purely emotional. She also responds on an intellectual level. Because the language of romance is more lushly symbolic and metaphorical than ordinary discourse, the reader is stimulated not only to feel, but also to analyze, interpret, and understand. Surveys of romance readers have consistently shown that these women are more highly educated and well-read than detractors have assumed, a fact which should be evident to anyone studying the mythological traditions underpinning the language of romance. When the heroine of Judith McNaught's *Whitney My Love* attends a ball costumed as Proserpina and meets a black-cloaked man whom she regards as "satanic" in appearance, the reader is expected to recognize the myth that is being alluded to and to identify this dark god as the novel's hero. Later in the novel when the heroine is forcibly carried off by this man, the reader understands that the story is following a map laid down by a far more ancient tale.

What exactly *is* the language of romance? For the purpose of discussion, we have decided to examine two forms of discourse: romantic dialogue and romantic description.

Dialogue in a romance novel serves a larger purpose than simply to provide exposition and demonstrate character. What is said between the hero and the heroine is often the primary battlefield for the conflicts between them. Provocative, confrontational dialogue has been the hallmark of the adversarial relationship that exists between the two major characters ever since the earliest days of romance narrative. It is Jayne Eyre's verbal impertinence that calls her to the attention of her employer, Mr. Rochester, who notes in one of their first conversations, "Ah! By my word! there is something singular about you . . . when one asks you a question, or makes a remark to which you are obliged to reply, you rap out a round rejoinder, which, if not blunt, is at least brusque." She is not his equal in terms of fortune or circumstance, but Jane proves early on that she is very much his equal in verbal acuity and assertiveness.

Such is also the case in *Pride and Prejudice,* in which Elizabeth Bennet's growing attraction for Mr. Darcy is based not only upon her "fine eyes," but also upon her ready wit. The opportunity to engage in verbal sparring is rarely declined by the heroines of romance since it is far more likely to be her words than her beauty that win her the love she most desires. Romances are full of heroes who eschew the company of beautiful but insipid women who would rather fawn than fight. Indeed, heroes of romance *enjoy* the duel of wits. Frequently they take the heroine's words to heart, changing in response to her stated criticisms. The heroine's words are her most potent weapon. It is Elizabeth's scathing refusal of his marriage proposal that forces Darcy to reevaluate his own behavior and relinquish the worst aspects of his pride; it is Cathy's overheard comment about Heathcliff's unsuitability as a husband that drives him from Wuthering Heights and inspires him to educate and improve himself.

In modern stories heroines continue to charm, provoke, and challenge their lovers with their conversation.

After only one spirited dialogue with Whitney Stone, the heroine of Judith McNaught's *Whitney My Love,* the Duke of Claymore is inspired to court her. "She had a sense of humor, an irreverent contempt for the absurd, that matched his own. She was warm and witty and elusive as a damned butterfly. She would never bore him as other women had."

In real life women often complain about the reluctance of their male partners to engage in meaningful dialogue, but in the world of romantic fantasy heroes willingly participate in verbal discussions. They fence, they flirt, they express their anger, they talk out the confounding details of their relationships with the heroine. No hero of romance will ever respond to the eternal feminine query, "What's wrong?" with the word, "Nothing." He will tell her what's wrong; they will argue about it, perhaps, but they will be communicating, and eventually, as they resolve their various conflicts, the war of words will end. One of the most significant victories the heroine achieves at the close of the novel is that the hero is able to express his love for her *not only physically but also verbally.* Don't just show me, tell me, is one of the prime messages that every romance hero must learn. Romance heroines, like women the world over, need to hear the words, and the dialogue of romance provides them with this welcome opportunity.

Our second form of discourse, romantic description, is frequently denounced by critics as being overly florid. But effusive imagery has a purpose. As we have already noted, the primary task of the romance writer is to create for her readers a vision of an alternative world and to give mythical dimension to its landscape and characters. Piling on the detail by means of a generous use of the romance codes is an effective way to achieve this goal. Lush use of symbols, metaphors, and allusion is emotionally powerful as well as mythologically evocative. It is the verbal equivalent of putting a person or an action under a microscope. Horror genre novelists like Stephen King use this technique to describe, for example, a murdered corpse, shocking the reader into a visceral response to the graphic horrors of death. Romance writers use the same technique in sensual love scenes to draw the reader into the landscape and to solidify her identification with the lovers by evoking within her some of the same emotions they are experiencing. The codes transport her to the world of romance and make her feel, briefly, as if she is a participant in the ancient dramas being enacted there.

The physical characteristics of the hero and heroine are presented in considerable detail, and phrases such as "his lean, hard thighs," "her sparkling, emerald eyes," "his penetrating glance," "her prim features were softened by a generous lower lip" are standard fare in romance. Many such codes reverberate with allusions to mythical archetypes: "He was leaning against the cold stone wall, regarding her steadily with a slight smile on his narrow, sensual lips. *Devil,* she thought" (Barlow, *Siren's Song*). And, from the hero in the same book: "Faerie music, he thought, listening to a low-toned feminine voice caressing the words of a ballad . . . this lovely Siren must be she."

A careful analysis of the physical description in most romance novels will demonstrate that, from a large lexicon of common descriptive codes, authors consciously or unconsciously choose those that best illustrate the particular archetypes with which they are working. Heroes associated with demons, the devil, the dark gods, and vampires tend to be dark-haired, with eyes that are luminous, piercing, penetrating, fierce, fiery, and so forth. Blond heroes are less common, but there is usually a fallen-angel quality about them.

In the passage of sample back cover copy at the beginning of this essay, the description of the hero is a blatant evocation of the Hades-Persephone myth. *Ravenwood* is dark and enigmatic, with the glittering eyes that one might expect to be attributed to the devil. He is clearly linked with the death god. Having drowned in the black, murky waters of a pond, the first Lady Ravenwood is a permanent shade in the underworld, and it is hinted that her husband may have been responsible.

Sophy is, in many ways, his opposite. Described as country bred, she is fresh and innocent. Like Persephone of the myth, she is drawn into a marriage that she does not, at first, desire. Her tawny hair, the color of wheat, evokes her role as the daughter of Demeter, the great earth goddess of the harvest, spring, fertility. Thus the descriptive language sets up one of the oldest and best-loved of romantic conflicts: the mythical battle of death and life, despair and hope, eternal darkness and everlasting light.

The individual words employed in the passage are highly connotative. Adjectives include such words as black, legendary, mysterious, beautiful, murky, country-bred, emerald, tawny-haired, and masculine. Verbs include whispered, drowned, drawn, burned, teach, love. Nouns include devil, wrath, waters, bride, lass, strength, desire, foul play, and marriage of convenience. Such language is emotionally loaded. Each word conjures up vivid images in the minds of the readers, and the combination of so many evocative phrases in a short passage of prose creates for the reader a dynamic, multi-layered intellectual and emotional gestalt.

Is it possible to do away with such language and still retain the romance? Suppose we tried to rewrite the passage in nonfigurative language. It might come out something like this:

> His acquaintances regard Julian, the Earl of Ravenwood, as neurotic. He's an odd character with a belligerent temperament, whose first wife drowned in the family swimming pool. Some believe she committed suicide, others think he murdered her.
>
> Sophy Dorring, an unsophisticated young woman, is engaged to Julian. Strongly attracted to him, she overcomes her initial reluctance to marry and sets her own agenda for their relationship: to help her husband get in touch with his emotions.

Same story, different language. But what a difference. By expressing the same ideas in ordinary discourse, we sacrifice the fantasy, the mythical elements, and that sense of magnificent opposition between two powerful but opposing forces. The problems of the hero and heroine are reduced to the mundane. Such diction might be deemed appropriate for the writer of mainstream fiction, but it is worthless to the romance novelist.

Another interesting detail about romantic description is the use of paradoxical elements, echoing the heavy use of paradoxical plot devices. Although the hero is more commonly associated with darkness, hardness, strength, roughness, and evil, and the heroine with light, softness, vulnerability, gentleness, and good, there are elements of strength in the heroine and softness in the hero. "A mouth that smiled easily was counterbalanced by the firm angles of her nose and jaw" (Krentz, *Affair of Honor*). "His eyes were large, brown, and dramatic . . . heavily fringed with dark lashes and arched with delicate brows that might have appeared too feminine had the rest of his features not been so uncompromisingly male" (Barlow, *Siren's Song*). Or, as the hero of Amanda Quick's *Seduction* notes about the heroine, "beneath that sweet, demure facade, she had a streak of willful pride."

The reason for this type of description is to distract the reader from the fantasy elements of the story long enough to remind her of the underlying reality of the hero's and heroine's characters. The hero is not really such a bad guy, the reader divines. And the heroine is much tougher and more self-sufficient than she initially appears.

Paradoxical words and phrases like "fierce pleasure" and "tender command" (from *Seduction*) are also used to depict the dynamics of the developing relationship. Frequently, the romance heroine is described as a "willing captive" to the "tender violence" of the hero's lovemaking. Detractors of the genre tend to quote such phrases to bolster their view that romance writers are doing a disservice to their sisters by perpetuating the myth that women enjoy rape. In reality, the rape of the heroine by the hero is rarely, if ever, seen in today's romance novel. Readers do not take such passages literally; indeed, the very use of paradox makes a literal interpretation impossible. The words "captive" and "violence" remind the reader of the ancient *fantasy* underpinning such tales—the Hades-Persephone myth, for example—while the function of the words "willing" and "tender" is to clue the reader in to the *reality* of the characters' lovemaking, which is consensual and loving.

The use of paradox also serves to hint at the perfect reconciliation that will occur at the end of the romance novel. This will be possible because each of the main characters is, in addition to being the embodiment of an ancient myth, a whole person, integrated and autonomous, with various strengths and weaknesses. When these two individuals come together, they create a union that is both mythological and real, a union that celebrates the power of the female to heal and civilize the male.

In conclusion, we suggest that in order to understand the appeal of romance fiction, one must be sensitive to the subtle codes, contained in figurative language and in plot, that point toward a uniquely feminine sharing of a common emotional and intellectual heritage. Dedicated romance readers, long accustomed to responding to these cues, perceive the hidden meanings intuitively and find through them an intimacy with other women all over the world. It is our sex, after all, that excels at reconciliation and intimacy. Recent works on the differences between men and women, whether these be biological, psychological, or linguistic, suggest that women's particular expertise seems to be our ability to form significant relationships with the men, women, and children in our lives and to anchor and hold these relationships together. The messages contained in romance fiction, the language in which these messages are conveyed, and the intense experience induced by the act of reading itself tend to support and reflect this essential feminine concern. Like a secret handshake, the codes make the reader feel that she is part of a group. They increase her feelings of connection to other women who share her most intimate thoughts, dreams, and fantasies.

In general, women tend to be less afraid than men to blend our voices with others. Women who write romance don't seek autonomy in our story-telling. We don't seek a distinctive voice (although most writers have one). Instead, in telling stories and using language that we *know* are beloved of women all over the world, we are validating each other. We are articulating the feelings and fantasies of our sisters who cannot, or choose not to, write them down. Their voices ring out, through us, as strongly as our own.

It may well be that the use of the romance codes are more important to the success of a particular romance novel than are the usual elements upon which fiction is judged—the logic and cleverness of the plot, the development of the characters, or the vigor and originality of the author's voice. It's interesting to note that what is usually regarded as "good" prose style—presupposing the value of the original, individual voice over the value of merged voices—is not necessary for the writing of romance. This is true because in romance novels the shared experience is more valuable than the independent one.

Is it possible that accepted literary standards of excellence are essentially patriarchal in nature? We propose this as a matter for further debate and discussion. Are there any differences between what men and women generally regard as acceptable prose style? Who made the rules that all serious writers are supposed to have internalized? "Get rid of every adjective and adverb," a male colleague advised me after reading a draft of my latest manuscript. He also advised the use of shorter sentences. Lean and spare, short and terse. No emotion.

But why, for example, must we show and not tell?

Women *enjoy* the telling. We value the exploration of emotion in verbal terms. We are not as interested in action as we are in depth of emotion. And we like the emotion to be clear and authoritative, not vague or overly subtle the way it often seems to be in male discourse.

Why do many of us who write romance feel a defiant pleasure as we compose our "bad" prose? Are we really a bunch of silly, incompetent, unoriginal writers, or are we thumbing our noses at the literary establishment while continuing to use the sort of diction that not only works best in our genre, but satisfies our most deep-seated fantasies on a subtle and profound level?

This is a subject upon which a good deal more could be written, and we hope, through this essay, to stimulate such debate. The greatest challenge for the romance writer working today is to excite and delight our readers while, at the same time, fulfilling their expectations. It has been our experience that this is best achieved by making full use of the codes and conventions that have served us well for centuries, codes that are universally recognized by our sisters in every nation and culture, codes that celebrate the most enduring myths of feminine consciousness.

LINDA BARLOW

Linda Barlow holds a B.A. and an M.A. in English literature. After seven years as a doctoral fellow and a lecturer in English at Boston College, Ms. Barlow put aside her dissertation on "Feminist Voices in Eighteenth and Nineteenth Century English Romances" to devote herself to a full-time career as a novelist.

Ms. Barlow has written ten books, including eight series romances for Berkley/Jove and Silhouette. Her historical romance *Fires of Destiny,* published by New American Library, appeared on the Waldenbooks mass market bestseller list. Her first hardcover novel, *Leaves of Fortune,* was published by Doubleday. Chosen as a main selection of the Doubleday Bookclub and an alternate selection of the Literary Guild, it was translated into foreign editions throughout the world. Among Ms. Barlow's numerous awards is the Golden Medallion from Romance Writers of America, which she won for *Leaves of Fortune. Her Sister's Keeper* was published by Warner in 1993.

LAURA KINSALE

The Androgynous Reader

Point of View in the Romance

It is a commonly accepted truism that when a woman reads a romance she is "identifying" with the heroine. Accusations directed at the genre, such as Marion Zimmer Bradley's (1990) polemic against romance, typically assume without further examination that a female reader must identify with the female lead and so is in danger of modeling her own life after a character who might be submissive, passive, or obsessed only with romantic love and maintaining her virginity. Academic analysts, not being writers of fiction, may perhaps be forgiven this rather superficial assumption about the reading experience, but romance authors—and, yes, even authors of sword and sorcery fantasy written for women, such as Bradley herself—often fall into the same error. So sure are they that the female reader must be identifying with the heroine that they create the character they suppose the modern, liberated woman must wish to be— so powerful in the corporation, so skilled at swordsmanship, so infallible with a rifle, talented at politics, tough-nosed in managing the ranch hands, invested with psychic powers, adroit with magic, highly educated, widely read, strong, smart, an excellent dancer and full of independent sass; in short, just the sort of person one would gladly strangle if one met her on the street.

Romance novels of this type have been known to succeed in the marketplace. The most obnoxiously "defiant beauty" will not necessarily ruin the effect of a romance. This is not because romance readers actually admire, or wish to be, defiant beauties. It is because the hero carries the book.

Kathleen Woodiwiss's *Shanna* (1977) provides a best-selling example. A sillier and more wrong-headed heroine than Shanna would be difficult to imagine; very few women would go to bed at night dreaming of actually resembling the annoying little shrew. Ah, but to be *in her place*—that is another matter.

That is what the heroine of this kind of romance represents: a placeholder. Feminists need not tremble for the reader—she does not identify with, admire, or internalize the characteristics of either a stupidly submissive or an irksomely independent heroine. The reader thinks about what she would have done in the heroine's place. The reader measures the heroine by a tough yardstick, asking the character to live up to the reader's standards, not vice versa.

Placeholding and reader identification should not be confused. Placeholding is an objective involvement; the reader rides along with the character, having the same experiences but accepting or rejecting the character's actions, words, and emotions on the basis of her personal yardstick. Reader identification is subjective: the reader *becomes* the character, feeling what she or he feels, experiencing the sensation of being *under control* of the character's awareness.

Even the most well-conceived and fascinating of romance heroines embodies an element of placeholding. However, it is myopic to believe that just because the reader is female she is confined to the heroine's character as the target of authentic reader identification.

In romance it is the hero who carries the book. Within the dynamics of reading a romance, the female reader *is* the hero, and also is the heroine-as-object-of-the-hero's-interest (the placeholder heroine). The reader very seldom *is* the heroine in the sense meant by the term "reader identification." There is always an element of analytical distance.

The reader is represented by and in competition with the heroine at the same time; therefore she has stiff requirements for this character, who must be presented as intelligent without being intimidating, independent without being offensive, attractive without being smug. No easy task for a writer (or for the contemporary liberated woman, for that matter) and one at which most of us have bombed all too frequently, unintentionally creating instead the "cast-iron bitches who appear petulant and unsympathetic rather than strong" that Jayne Ann Krentz (1990) has warned us about. When the writer does fail with the heroine, however, it is quite easy for the reader to disassociate herself from the character and continue to derive pleasure from the story by using the heroine as placeholder.

Tania Modleski's (1982) analysis of how third person point of view works, supposing it to be merely a sort of convenience—no more than first person narrative with "schizophrenic" asides to the audience—and claiming that "hardly any critical distance is established between reader and [heroine]," manages not only to overlook the power of third person narrative in controlling and creating emotion and reader identification but to get everything backwards. The first and most deceptively simple rule every toddling writer learns is Show and Don't Tell. The next thing the writer learns is just how difficult that standard is to achieve, particularly when trying to Show rather than Tell something about a character while in that character's consciousness. It is not an impossible thing to do by any means, but it is an enduring challenge. We all fall back on telling, and Modleski's "schizophrenic narrator," the "man-watching-from-the-closet" who makes omniscient comments about the heroine's beauty, is really just an untalented writer. From Jane Austen to James Joyce, it is not only the finely turned phrase but the well-chosen *showing* that is truly vivid, dragging the spectator into the character's existence by creating a spontaneous, unforced, uninhibited transfer of feeling, character-reader-character.

In a romance written from the heroine's third person viewpoint, who is most often being effectively shown in this intense kind of character evocation?

The hero.

The heroine's third person point of view is as likely to create distance between reader and heroine as to close it, especially in the hands of a mediocre writer who relies on beating the reader over the head with direct information about a character from within that character's viewpoint. In general, rather than identifying with the heroine, the romance reader is probably farther from truly enmeshing her emotions and personality with those of the heroine than of any other significant character.

It is strange that so little note has been taken of this phenomenon. Perhaps the point has been overlooked because analysts have focused so narrowly on reports from readers. The underlying effect of viewpoint is not obvious to the average reader, who, if asked, simply equates point of view with reader identification, assuming that if the writer has put her in a character's viewpoint, she must be "identifying" with that character, when in fact her strongest emotional response may well be engendered by a different source: the viewed actions of another character. In the context of this mistaken equation of viewpoint and emotional identification, Carol Thurston's (1987) early- and mid-1980s reader surveys both showed not only a striking aversion to the heroine-only point of view but an avid desire for the hero's. Thurston describes the results as a desire for a "mixed" point of view, but the only applicable question on her first survey appears to be: "Would you like to read stories written from the hero's point of view?"

I don't see anything remotely "mixed" about the question or about a 70 percent positive response to it in 1982. If one considers the very real possibility that, by desiring the hero's "point of view" in such an overwhelming majority, these readers are actually asking for emotional identification with the hero, not simply his viewpoint, the response is a plain rejection of heroine-identification in favor of hero-identification. Thurston probes around the edges of the issue, pointing out that "Readers are no longer satisfied with seeing only how the New Hero responds, they now want to look inside his head," but doesn't seem to confront the fact that romance readers have never had any intention of stopping so short as a mere look.

I should reemphasize that the intensity of hero-identification is not necessarily predicted by the actual point of view in which the novel is written. A skillful writer can achieve a high degree of character revelation and reader identification with the hero without ever entering the hero's point of view. A truly great romance writer can even do it within the heroine's first person narrative: *Jane Eyre* is the classic example. However, it is certainly simpler—though not always more effective—for us mere mortals to invoke the reader's powerful stake in the hero by using his viewpoint. To be honest, female romance writers seem to be more talented at Showing and Not Telling for the male lead than for the female, even from within his point of view (all those years of dealing with the strong, silent type, I guess). We had better be good at it, because our survival in the genre rides on how well we actuate the hero.

Indeed, until the 1980s, writers of Harlequin romances had to struggle to maintain clear and vivid "internalizable" heroes without entering the male point of view. At that time, authors were actually prevented from using the male viewpoint by their publishers, who clearly operated solidly within the idea that the reader always identifies with the heroine. The difficulty in meeting the imperative of providing sufficiently evocable and illuminated heroes was obviously of critical concern to readers, who have repeatedly called for more books "from the hero's point of view" (Macro, 1989).

Significantly, now that the trend has swung firmly toward a substantial dose of masculine viewpoint, we hear no cries at all for "more of the heroine's point of view." In my own historical romance, *The Prince of Midnight*, the heroine's character is virtually inaccessible for almost half the book, with little of her viewpoint and less explanation of it. The only comments I received from readers on the topic were complaints that they were frustrated *on behalf of the hero* because the heroine treated him so coolly. Because this same frustration was one of the hero's dominant emotions in the course of the book, I am led to the conclusion that these readers were comfortably identifying with him, not her.

Through her own and the hero's eyes, the reader watches and judges the heroine; the reader does not typically *become* the heroine in the way she often *becomes* the hero as she reads, although the closer she moves toward spontaneously identifying with both hero and heroine the more rich and rewarding the romance is likely to be for her. When placeholder and reader identification merge, the experience of the story is utterly absorbing and vital; analytical distance recedes; the book becomes, as Janice Radway (1984, p. 64) has suggested, "not merely the events of a courtship but *what it feels like*" (emphasis Radway's).

If Radway had stopped there, she would have been close to the heart of the matter, but she goes on to say "*what it feels like* to be the *object* of one, though this need not be accomplished by telling the story solely from the heroine's point of view." Radway's own italics in this second quote highlight where it is that she falls victim to the belief that the female reader is identifying only with the heroine, whether or not in the heroine's point of view. Although the readers she interviewed "admitted that they want to identify with the heroine," what she describes them doing in this identification sounds to me like using the heroine as placeholder.

If one begins with and proceeds from the presumption of heroine-identification, looking neither right nor left, everything female readers say about the reading experience is colored in that light, and subtle—or perhaps not so subtle—realities are neglected.

My readers' voices come through loud and clear in letters, emphasizing a different perspective. "Please, *please* write more books from the man's point of view." "So many of the books dwell on the heroine, but the men are rather vague." "All too often, because these novels are written by women for women, there's an inability to probe the male psyche beyond the he-has-to-be-strong-and-can't-emote scenario." "Since I began to read romances in 1972, I've longed for more hero point of view." "If [the hero] isn't in the first chapter or two, I'll put the book down. It's just boring."

Of course, there can't be a love story (a heterosexual love story, anyway) without a hero, and complaints such as these are usually interpreted to mean that the romance is missing until the hero shows up. But I propose that, for a large proportion of romance readers, there's much more to the male character than half of the romantic relationship. When Radway says, "The focus never shifts for these readers away from the woman at the center of the romance," I think she is wrong. One hundred percent dead blind wrong. I flatly believe that *the man carries the book.*

Naturally, I have my own hunches about why the chemistry of reading a romance is so heavily weighted toward the male character. It is fairly obvious that the bottom line is sexual admiration: to me, a large part of it feels like a simple, erotic, and free-hearted female joy in the very existence of desirable maleness. Hey, women *like* men.

The pivotal twist on this commonplace observation, and something that seems to have been generally disregarded, is the significance of preferential hero-identification. What does it mean to a woman to feel—to want keenly to feel—what the male character feels as she reads?

I think that, as she identifies with a hero, a woman can become what she takes joy in, can realize the maleness in herself, can experience the sensation of living inside a body suffused with masculine power and grace (adjectives very commonly applied to heroes, including my own), can explore anger and ruthlessness and passion and pride and honor and gentleness and vulnerability: yes, ma'am, all those old romantic clichés. In short, she can *be* a man.

A fictional man, that is. I'm not speaking here of some male malarkey about penis envy (penis envy being a concept that causes the average woman to wrinkle her nose and say, "What?"). Identifying with a fictional hero is quite a different thing from wishing to be a real-life male or trying to control one, because this fictional man is altogether within and part of the reader herself: a vigorous, living aspect of her personality. He may be fictitious with regard to genuine males (and only the most oblivious of women wouldn't know it), but he exists nevertheless.

Many readers comment that their husbands or boyfriends are leery of romance novels, bewildered by female enjoyment of the books, and really quite frightened that they're being put in competition with and held up to the standard of fictional heroes. It is logical to assume that much of the negative male reaction to the romance genre is based on this alarm. Who wouldn't worry?

But fictional characters, as real as they can seem, are entirely internal constructs within the reader: the whole adventure is an interior one. A novel that works, in which reader identification takes place, is a methodical realization of elements of the reader's innermost life. If the taproot isn't there in the reader in the first place, the novel will not tap anything. The reader reads a good novel with a sense of discovery, but it is a discovery of elements of the existing inner self. Many of the old epic myths seem confusing and strange to modern readers, not because the mythical elements aren't still alive in the human psyche but because the telephone lines are down, the expression is too foreign, the connection—the self-discovery—doesn't get made. So, as Ann Maxwell and Jayne Ann Krentz (1989) have so clearly revealed, we rewrite the myths and make the journey in our own time and vernacular.

While I accept this idea that the romance genre perpetuates the archetypal myths, I think there is yet a deeper level at which women experience romance novels. Those poor boyfriends and spouses trembling in their boots can take comfort. They're scared of phantoms. A romance reader is not expecting any real-life person to live up to the heroes of her novels. She is experiencing herself as hero, and as heroine, completely within her own personality. If a hero or heroine does something the reader would not do, she will reject it. If she likes the character enough, she will pretend it didn't happen and go on; if she doesn't, across the room the book flies. If either hero or heroine does something she would admire herself for doing, she is warmed in an internal way: "This is good, this is right, this is *me.*"

But regarding the heroine there is still, and always, that element of not-me, of her, of otherness. There is paradox involved in the placeholding component of the heroine. The reader is female in reality; therefore, it requires a greater stretch, a maximum submersion and letting go of self, to *be* another woman: the fundamental identity of gender means that a reader prefers not to surrender too much of her own individuality to this character but to remain judiciously objective. I suspect it is this sensation that Modleski is labeling "hysteria," "hypocrisy," "schizophrenia," and "bad faith" in her description of the romance reader's experience of what I would call placeholding, a phenomenon that seems to me to be the exact opposite: a healthy maintenance of separate self-identity while reading fiction. If one can bring oneself to admit that a female reader might find it more difficult to *be* this fictitious heroine than to *be* this fictitious man—not because she is a pitiful, victimized woman but because within the reader there are masculine elements that can and need to be realized—then reading a romance is far from internally alienating. It is integrating. It is satisfying. It is downright fun, in fact.

What reading a romance becomes, then, is the experience of "what a courtship feels like," but a courtship carried on entirely between myself and myself. This heroine is holding my place (or perhaps I even like her enough to identify with her to an extent) and I am the hero. That is why romance readers are not, and never have been, intimidated by what Krentz calls the "alpha male" hero, the "retrograde, old-fashioned, macho, hard-edged man"—because the alpha male hero is themselves.

In the reading of a romance, the conflict and resolution of a romantic relationship are entirely within the reader and have nothing directly to do with the reader's husband, boyfriend, male boss, or male co-workers, except as they may interfere with the reading process itself. If, as Krentz suggests, the romantic male lead always represents both hero and villain, then the reader must be experiencing those aspects of herself. If the hero is being gentled and tamed, it is a taming and gentling of passions *within the female reader,* not within any real-life male. Experienced and mentally healthy fiction readers always know where the fable ends and actuality begins. Reading a romance is not practice for the real thing. As Maxwell and Krentz say, "We do not read . . . for a reality check."

Not an external reality check, at any rate, but perhaps an internal one. I suspect that for a woman a romance may be a working-through of her own interior conflicts and passions, her own "maleness" if you will, that resists and resists giving in to what is desired above all, and yet feared above all, and then, after the decisive climax, arrives at a resolution, a choice that carries with it the relief and pleasure of internal harmony.

The oft-derided happy ending is no infantile regressive daydream; it is a dramatization of the integration of the inner self, an integration that goes on day by day, moment by moment, in the lives of women and men all over the world, because—yes—civilization and family and growing up require of all of us, male *and* female, a certain turning away from adventure, from autonomy, from what-might-have-been, and we mourn the loss and must deal with it. (Romance novels aren't the only manifestation of this fact. Pro football, male buddy movies, and men's genre fiction exist for a reason.) A female attorney, mother of three, who represents a labor union and reads and writes romance—a working *attorney* and *mother,* mind you, a modern superwoman— writes, "I have a very strong vision of what I might have been had I not 'settled down' and gotten married . . . and I spend a considerable amount of psychological time and energy wrestling with it. This has nothing to do with my relationship with my husband, my children or dominance in my marriage. IT HAS TO DO WITH MYSELF. The choice [of marriage and family] is my choice, quite freely made, but often regretted nevertheless. Romances express that ambivalence, and then come down solidly on the side of getting married."

That tired old claim that romance is not real literature because "happy endings aren't realistic" is silly, not to say pigheadedly obtuse. Romances have happy endings and the hero never dies in them because literature as represented by the romance genre expresses integration, not fractionalization, of the self. And in particular, I am convinced, romance reflects the exploration and reconciliation of male elements within the female reader.

I believe that feminism may have taken something of a false step with many women when the more zealous constituents of the movement insisted upon placing "femaleness" in direct opposition to "maleness"—a bias well illustrated in Bradley's selection of short stories for her sword and sorcery collections, in which the females consistently outperform, outsmart, and out-philosophize the sorry collection of males they are arrayed against: so often *against,* with winners and losers.

Perhaps this sort of thing is a hangover from an earlier, more desperate phase of feminism; but still, I think a large number of women simply never did require a devaluation of male characteristics. What they savor instead is the freedom to expand into all the aspects, feminine and masculine, of their own being. As the attorney cited above puts it, "we like the male inside ourselves."

To wheedle authentic reader identification out of a

heroine is one of the toughest tasks a romance writer faces, and it is by no means her most important one. A heroine who is true to herself, whatever her self may be—jet pilot or bashful spinster—is enough to make her part in the mechanics of a romance workable, if not a work of art. I am *not* proposing that authors shouldn't bother to create convincing heroines; indeed we should, and must. What I am saying is that in the rank order of reader interest and identification, the heroine always falls second to the hero—a property as integral to the romance as fourteen lines of five-foot iambic rhyme is integral to the sonnet.

As the author of the first (to my knowledge) historical romance to have the hero alone on the cover, I have had a ringside seat at this new twist in the romance genre. It has been well known for some time among romance writers that many readers are rebelling against the standard "clinch" covers of historicals, with particular complaints voiced about the over-endowment of the illustrated females. The persistence of the clinch cover goes beyond market identification and the subconscious appeal of pornographic illustrations of females to male wholesale book buyers (a penchant rather amusingly hinted at in the very real and serious apprehension of two male buyers with whom I spoke about *The Prince of Midnight*'s hero-only cut-back cover: "But where's the girl?" "I like the inside [a ripping-off-of-her-dress-and-crawling-in-the-guy's-lap clinch] better"). It is also another example of the fallacy of heroine-identification: everyone—publishers, art directors, and book buyers included—has been convinced that readers are identifying with the heroine; therefore the illustrated heroine should be gorgeous and well endowed, because that is what all women wish to be, right?

Wrong.

At first, like everyone else, I attributed the enormous popularity of *The Prince of Midnight*'s hero-only cover to the fact that romance readers are sick and tired of illustrations that focus so heavily on something in which they have no interest whatsoever—big-breasted, lust-crazed women—and are ready and waiting for a cover that emphasizes something in which they are highly interested: a hunk.

I believe now that the issue is not so simple. That interpretation is certainly valid, but hunks have graced the covers of romances before—the very same hunk in fact, male model Fabio, as on *The Prince of Midnight*—and while these covers have been popular and sold well, they have not created the stir of comment within the genre that the hero-only cover created.

It is possible that, by delivering an attractive illustration of the hero alone, the publisher is doing more than merely furnishing the female reader with something concrete on which to hang the fantasy, in the way a Playboy centerfold provides a hook for a man's sexual fantasy. While I do believe this is a strong element in the success of the hero-only cover, a hero-only illustration may also serve to reinforce and enhance the reader's ability to identify with this man. The visual experience is not so fluid as the reading experience: the presence of a heroine in the illustration is rock-solid evidence that this character is *not* "me," and cannot be "me," because there she is, somebody else, right on the cover. On the other hand, when the reader has the hero alone on the cover, not only can she hold her own place as heroine but the cover message agrees with her perception of who is the real center of this book.

Perhaps the most intriguing conundrum of hero-identification is the joy romance readers take in the "fractured hero": the ripped-up, torn apart, brought-to-his-knees alpha male. Once again, this is a phenomenon that has been widely interpreted in the light of presumed heroine-identification. Modleski has argued that it represents a female revenge fantasy: ". . . all the while [the hero] is being so hateful, he is internally grovelling, grovelling, grovelling." Others have emphasized, like Krentz, the mythic struggle of the female to civilize and bond to the male or, like Radway, the creation of a comforting fairy tale of perfect romantic love. In these interpretations an emotionally shattered hero presumably would be a tamed one, providing for the reader the vicarious satisfaction of the heroine's success.

Perhaps so. But I would like to point out one salient fact. During the height of the reading experience—the romantic climax—when the reader feels that wrench of emotion, the tingle in the spine, the full and authentic inner twist of reader identification with a character in an emotional cataclysm—when Rhett says to Scarlett, "Frankly, my dear . . ."; when Ruark Beauchamp of *Shanna* raises an inhuman "raging howl . . . from the wagon accompanied by repeated thuds against the heavy wooden door"; when Clayton Westmoreland shatters the brandy glass in his hand in Judith Mc-Naught's *Whitney My Love;* when Slade in Nora Roberts's *A Matter of Choice* growls, "I love you, damn it. I'd like to choke you for it"—*who,* may I ask, *is* the reader at that moment?

Not the heroine, basking in female revenge or bonding triumph.

Oh, no. She's the hero.

REFERENCES

Bradley, Marion Zimmer. 1990. "Introduction." In Bradley, ed., *Sword and Sorceress VI: An Anthology of Heroic Fantasy*, pp. 7–10. New York: DAW Books.

Kinsale, Laura. 1990. *The Prince of Midnight*. New York: Avon Books.

Krentz, Jayne Ann. 1990. "The Alpha Male." *Romance Writers Report* 10, 1: 26–28.

Macro, Lucia. 1989. "Heroes for Our Time: Silhouette Desire Announces 1989 Is the Year of the Man." *Romance Writers Report* 9, 1:43.

Maxwell, Ann and Jayne Ann Krentz. 1989. "The Wellsprings of Romance." *Romance Writers Report* 9, 5: 21–23.

McNaught, Judith. 1985. *Whitney My Love*. New York: Pocket Books.

Modleski, Tania. 1982. *Loving with a Vengeance: Mass Produced Fantasies for Women*. Hamden, CT: Archon Books.

Radway, Janice. 1984. *Reading the Romance: Women, Patriarchy, and Popular Literature*. Chapel Hill: University of North Carolina Press.

Roberts, Nora. 1984. *A Matter of Choice*. Silhouette Intimate Moments #49. New York: Silhouette Books.

Thurston, Carol. 1987. *The Romance Revolution: Erotic Novels for Women and the Quest for a New Sexual Identity*. Urbana: University of Illinois Press.

Woodiwiss, Kathleen. 1977. *Shanna*. New York: Avon Books.

Various personal communications by letter or telephone, 1987–91.

LAURA KINSALE

Laura Kinsale's 1990 historical romance *The Prince of Midnight* was voted Best Book of the Year by the Romance Writers of America, while her most recent novel, *The Shadow and the Star,* has been nominated for the same award and appeared on the *New York Times,* Waldenbooks, B. Dalton, Barnes and Noble, and Ingram mass market bestseller lists. Her five earlier historical romances have received numerous awards from romance trade magazines and organizations of fans. She is a former uranium and petroleum geologist with a Master of Science degree from the University of Texas at Austin.

LINDA BARLOW

The Androgynous Writer

Another View of Point of View

During the period when I was writing my historical romance novel *Fires of Destiny* I had a recurring dream in which Roger Trevor, the hero, would appear on my doorstep, saber rattling, to complain that I was allowing my feminist sensibilities to subvert his original rough, tough, macho character.

"The more you perfect your bloody little fairy tale, the more of a lily-livered wimp I turn out to be," says he.

"You're becoming a more mature, civilized, and sympathetic hero," I assure him.

"Yeah, well I liked it better when I dragged the heroine off to my ship at knifepoint and ravished her."

Truth is, despite my feminist qualms, so did I.

I'm not ashamed to admit that I've always been one of those die-hard fans of the old-fashioned, hard-edged romances which feature a feisty heroine who falls into love and conflict with a dangerous hero with sardonic eyebrows and a cruel but sensual mouth. In the romances I most enjoy, as well as the ones I write, the intensity of excitement I feel while reading is directly proportional to the level of emotional hazard the heroine experiences as her relationship with the hero develops. When he stalks her, carries her off, besieges her honor, and finally makes love to her with a passion and determination that would unnerve me if I ever encountered it in real life, I greedily turn the pages, finding within such scenes a catharsis of the essential impulse or desire that led me to pick up the book in the first place.

Why? That's a tough one. I love "serious" literature, which I studied and taught, first as a graduate student and subsequently as a lecturer in English at Boston College before I became a published romance novelist. When I first switched careers, I used to feel vaguely guilty that my time, which ought to be spent in the serious study of Shakespeare, Austen, Virginia Woolf, or Charlotte Perkins Gilman, was now committed to the creation of pulse-pounding works of popular women's fiction that rework the most ancient myths about the relations of men and women.

But I have come to believe that the enduring popularity of the romance novel through time and across all boundaries of nation and culture proves that the appeal of such narratives reverberates on the deepest levels of feminine understanding. Romances are the stories that women tell to themselves . . . and to each other. Whether they be passionately metaphorical in the manner of Charlotte Brontë, witty and ironical in the manner of Jane Austen, or imperfectly rendered in the purplest of prose, they are the voices of women, bravely upraised. It is time these voices were heard, acknowledged, and understood.

Although I have read several fascinating essays on romance novels as political or cultural documents, I see them as psychological maps which provide intriguing insights into the emotional landscape of women. The various elements contained in them function as internal archetypes within the feminine psyche. This includes the hero, whom I see not as the masculine object of feminine consciousness but as a significant aspect of feminine consciousness itself.

In the most traditional sense, the romance novel is an emotional coming-of-age story. At some subliminal level, the narrative teaches a woman how to reconcile the various aspects of her own psyche that may be at war with one another so that she can feel herself to be a truly integrated, competent, and emotionally whole individual who is able to perform her various functions in the world.

Psychologically, the fundamental romance novel situation—woman and man meet in an atmosphere of intense attraction and conflict that is eventually transformed by the conciliatory power of love into a lasting pair bond—may be the nearest thing a woman has to the oedipal myth that allows the male to separate from his mother and establish his autonomous adult personality. Psychologists have begun to recognize that women do not make this separation so easily and that, indeed, it is not autonomy but intimacy that is valued by many women. On a profound level, the romantic myth enables us to comprehend the inner forces that must be manipulated in order to gain the confidence and the competence necessary to fulfill our vital task of negotiating successful relationships with the men, women, and children in our lives.

How does the map work and what directions is it providing? Although we are currently seeing an extraordinary diversity in the themes, plots, and characterizations in romance novels, all romances share four basic elements: a heroine, a hero, a conflict-ridden love story, and a happily-ever-after ending. Because in the best of these stories both the conflict and the resolution derive from the characters of the lovers themselves, it is upon them that I will focus.

The romance heroine is the primary aspect of feminine consciousness, the character with whom the reader is most likely to identify. She is engaging and likable, a genuinely sympathetic character. If she does more reacting than acting, more responding than initiating, this is hardly a surprise since it is with this aspect of femininity that most women are comfortable. Many of us were not brought up to be initiators; we have had to struggle for years, not only with other people's expectations of what we are capable of achieving but also with our own internal expectations. At a women's gathering I recently attended, each participant was asked to cast away the one thing in life that she felt was holding her back. Eleven of the twelve women present cast away some sort of fear—fear of losing control, fear of not being able to take care of themselves, fear of expressing their true feelings, fear of using their natural gifts in the most productive way, fear of husbands and lovers, fear of disappointing the people they most love. Given our long heritage of patriarchically induced feminine anxieties, it is natural for women to identify with the character who, at the beginning of the romance, may seem to lack her full complement of power and authority.

Despite our instinctive identification with the heroine, most of us know that we are not subservient by nature. Recent archaeological studies have suggested that feminine passivity was by no means the norm in ancient cultures, and that the first religious practices were dominated by images of the Great Goddess rather than a masculine god. The Mother is a potent and terrifying figure—male and female we come forth from Her and are swallowed up by Her again in the end; Hers is the awesome power both of life and of death. But the full power of the goddess is not available to women in the early stages of life. In Everywoman's journey through the three primary aspects of the goddess—virgin to mother to crone—the romance novel maps out the first segment of the journey. And like any archetypal journey it is filled with threats and dangers against which the heroine must struggle and eventually prevail.

And she does prevail. Although there may be a great deal of variation from book to book as to the personal characteristics of the heroine, all these women share one vital quality—courage. The feistiness of the heroine is so universal as to have become a cliché. She does not fall apart in a crisis in the manner that we might imagine ourselves doing. She copes. She determines ways to extract herself from the disasters—both physical and emotional—that threaten her. How does she accomplish this? By casting away her fears, facing her demons, and taking the actions that initiate her into her own considerable power.

The most formidable of her demons is, of course, the hero. He is also the demon of many commentators who attempt to defend the romance novel. If romances are really about female empowerment rather than masculine domination, why do so many of them continue to regale their readers with so much blatant, undifferentiated machismo?

In my opinion, they don't. The machismo is something of an illusion.

Traditionally, the hero is the Byronic type—dark and brooding, writhing inside with all the residual anguish of his shadowed past, world-weary and cynical, quick-tempered and prone to fits of guilt and depression. He is strong, virile, powerful, and lost. Adept at many things that carry with them the respect and admiration of the world (particularly the world of other males), he is not fully competent in the arena where women excel—the arena of his emotions, which are violently out of control.

Is this really the sort of man most women want? Of course not. Even as a young adolescent reading my first romances, I can't remember ever feeling that the fictional representation I was encountering had much to do with the real *external* world. I didn't expect to meet and marry the man of my fantasies; indeed, the warm, loving, even-tempered man I did marry has little in common with the brooding hero of romance. Instead, almost from the beginning, I identified with the hero. I saw him as Self, not Other. And I dimly recognized him as one of the archetypal figures in my own inner landscape.

The romantic hero is *not* the feminine ideal of what a man should be. The romantic hero, in fact, is not a man at all. He is a split-off portion of the heroine's own psyche which will be reintegrated at the end of the book.

In the best romances, we are just as emotionally engaged with the hero as we are with the heroine. We feel his anger and understand his pain. And we sense that the reason the heroine is so powerfully attracted to him, despite his many faults, is that he is her shadow—the dark side of herself that she denies and projects outward. It has been argued that psychological integration depends on encountering the shadow and accepting it. If the romance novel teaches a woman to love anybody, the person she must learn to love is herself.

If the heroine's primary role in the myth serves to encourage us to cope with our fears, the hero's is to provide us with the means of facing and accepting the angry, aggressive, sexually charged components of our personality that we have been taught to associate with masculinity. From childhood, males have more outlets for their aggressions—sports, horseplay, roughhousing, the rite of passage schoolyard fight and resultant black eye that parents (especially fathers) seem willing to tolerate. They also have more outlets for their sexuality, the expression of which is not only tolerated but encouraged. Females, on the other hand, are instructed from childhood to control, repress, or even split off their aggressive and erotic drives. Where does all that energy go? The temptation to generalize is strong, but here I will speak only for myself.

I was thirteen years old when I created the above-mentioned Roger Trevor, the first and most interesting of my various romantic heroes. Initially he was not an erotic figure; he was more villain than hero. A contemporary of the heroine's father, he did not threaten her honor but rather her life.

In a subsequent version of the story, written while I was in my late teens and early twenties, Roger's anger and eroticism are both blatant and entwined. He is violent, capable of killing (if only in self-defense). His treatment of Alexandra, the heroine, is charged with sexual energy, although he believes her to be too young, too sweet, too *good* for him. In a plot twist that many fans of the bodice ripper will recognize, Roger becomes convinced that Alexandra "is not what she seems," and in an explosion of rage that I relished describing since it went so far beyond the scope of any anger I permitted myself, he descends to rape. Alexandra's response to his violence is a frozen rather than an awakened sexuality, and for the rest of the novel a guilt-stricken Roger must do harsh penance as he attempts to reengage her desire and her love.

Although I never tried to sell this early version of my narrative, I became obsessed by Roger Trevor. He was always storming about in my head. Although his violence puzzled me and his actions made me feel guilty, I continued to write and rewrite his story. Why was he so important to me?

It took me several years to understand and accept that I had become adept at repressing most of the anger that Roger was so quick to display. I was resentfully submissive in situations where I would have preferred to be dominant. I was restrained and polite where I would much rather have been straightforward and honest. He represented the darker side of myself, the powerful male figure on whom I was projecting all my own aggressiveness and rage. As a male, he could do the things that had been traditionally forbidden to me. He personified the freer, wilder, more libidinous sides of myself. On some deep level, I *was* Roger.

A curious thing happened as I began writing the final version of my novel. As I became more accepting of my own negative emotions, Roger became more civilized. Although he remained a dangerous hero, suspected of murder, potentially capable of rape, some of his aggressiveness began to shift subtly to Alexandra. In the published romance, it is she who loves and desires Roger, she who eagerly responds to his initial advances, she who yearns for the relationship that he is actively resisting. When the twists of the plot finally inspire his old rapist's rage, the feisty Alexandra loses her temper as well and orders *him* down on the bed. The sexual encounter that follows is not violent but mutually satisfactory, the lovemaking of two adults. Alexandra does not "become" a woman in this scene, she already is a woman, confident and assertive, able both to defuse the anger of her lover and to demand erotic pleasure for herself.

If Roger's and Alexandra's story is in any way representative, the romantic hero serves as the means by which the anxious but courageous heroine is initiated into *her own* aggressive and erotic tendencies, which are essential to her mature humanity. She experiences sex, or, in the case of many of the more modern romances in which she has previous sexual experience, she enjoys a hitherto unknown level of eroticism. She also experiences anger (his, as well as her own defiant response to his rage) and learns that both experiences are not only survivable but liberating in some way. She forms a spiritual union with the hero, sharing his masculine erotic and aggressive energy, becoming one with him—his other half, his soulmate. The marriage at the end is far more than a simple societal convention; it is the integration of the no-longer-a-girl's personality. She no longer needs to split off the forbidden portions of her own personality. The displaced voice of the hero is now her own voice, ringing with feminine force and vitality.

Romances must end at this point. If the heroine were to continue to increase in her own power and authority she would see that once the passage from virgin to mother is accomplished, men, in a way, are no longer essential. The virgin, almost by definition, requires a male partner in order to move into the second aspect of the goddess, but in women's narratives that deal with motherhood, midlife, and aging, men are less central to the myth.

If the romance novel is indeed a mythical playing out of Everywoman's archetypal journey toward psychological integration, this may explain why male readers and reviewers have responded so negative to the genre (unfortunately, the same might be said of male-trained female critics): they simply don't get it. The fundamental appeal of the romance novel escapes them because they cannot read the signposts or walk the road. They are foreigners in our emotional landscape.

What we are dealing with in romance novels is the inner material of feminine consciousness, passionately and defiantly expressed by women who have been oppressed and repressed by the forms and strictures of the patriarchy. Because of the deep-seated nature of this material, the romantic myth will continue to be dreamed and explored by women, and hard-eyed heroes will continue to rage against the plucky heroines who defy them until they are forever united by the reconciling power of love.

SUSAN ELIZABETH PHILLIPS

The Romance and the Empowerment of Women

In the late 1970s I was living in a suburban New Jersey community, an area of station wagons and crabgrass-free lawns. I had abandoned my teaching career six years earlier to stay at home and raise our two sons. When a new neighbor moved with her family into a house two doors away, we quickly formed a solid friendship, and one of the foundations of that friendship was our love of reading. Between nursery school car pools and trips to the grocery store, we discussed the books we loved, from the classics to the latest bestsellers.

At this time the paperback original historical romance was gaining huge popularity, and we fell under its spell. Gradually, we began bypassing John Updike for Kathleen Woodiwiss and Jennifer Wilde. The historical romances of this period were sometimes labeled "bodice rippers," not without a certain justification since many of them contained narrow-eyed heroes who smoked thin cheroots, were perpetually sardonic, and committed some rather violent sex acts on the heroines.

In this current era of the politically correct, I would love to say that we were horrified by these acts of violence against women, that we picketed bookstores and wrote outraged letters to publishers. But neither of us had ever been a victim of violence, and the undeniable fact is . . .

We loved these books.

We loved them despite the fact that we were the two most outspoken feminists in our neighborhood. College educated, opinionated, and aggressive, we sniffed out male chauvinism in everyday life like ever-zealous bloodhounds. God help any unsuspecting male who called out "Hello, girls!" when we took our evening walks. We worried about women who didn't take command of their lives. We voted for political candidates who championed women's rights. And we made our husbands' lives miserable if they didn't display the appropriate amount of gratitude for the fact that we had put our professional lives on hold to raise their children.

We saw no conflict between our feminist views and the content of the books we were reading. I can't remember that we even mentioned it, and if we did, our analysis would almost certainly have fallen under the category of "Fiction is fiction and real life is real life." The books were fun to read. They blocked out squabbling children and boring household chores. That was all.

The years passed and I became a published writer, producing two historical romances and then entering the world of women's mainstream popular fiction. Since 1983 when my first book was published, I have participated in countless discussions with both readers and my peers about the phenomenal appeal of the romance novel. For years, the consensus of opinion has been that we offered readers an escape from reality through the fantasy of an exciting man, a glamorous setting, a wonderful adventure. We were entertainers.

Ah, yes. Entertainers. That sounded good to me.

By the late 1980s, my life had grown increasingly stressful. My writing career had moved into high gear. I had two active sons and a husband who was frequently out of town on business. I was becoming a statistic—another overworked, overstressed, two-career American woman. I found myself awakening in the middle of the night with my heart pounding and nightmare visions of the insurance bill I had forgotten to pay, the plot line in my newest book that wasn't working out, the child who was being teased on the school bus. I would lie in bed staring at the ceiling while I made lists in my head of the things I had to do.

I seemed to have lost my ability to relax except late in the evenings when I would grab a romance novel. But instead of picking up a big mainstream book of women's fiction such as the ones I was writing myself, books that tended to be less formulaic and more complex in their depiction of male/female relationships, I was curling up with traditional historical romances or short contemporary series romances by authors such as Sandra Brown, Janet Dailey, Jayne Ann Krentz, Elizabeth Lowell, and Judith McNaught. I didn't have to read for long before something magical happened. I felt better. Calmer. In control.

Gradually, I began to realize that the romance novel was providing me with a fantasy of which I was very much in need. But it wasn't the fantasy that I had always assumed romance writers were offering their readers—that of a wonderful man or a glamorous, fulfilling career. *I already had those things.* Instead, the fantasy these novels offered me was one of command and control over the harum scarum events of my life—a fantasy of female empowerment.

For me, there was nothing more satisfying than the illusion that I was in command of all the external forces that so frequently frazzled and threatened me in real life, and as I talked to other women, both writers and readers, it became evident that I wasn't the only one experiencing this feeling. I began to ask myself how the romance novel provided this fantasy of empowerment. And why did women need it?

The answer to this latter question seemed to me the most obvious. Biologically, we are the weaker sex. We bear children, but because we do not have the physical strength that men do, we are never certain of our ability to protect them from harm. Newspaper headlines scream of rapes, murders, and mutilations. We are bombarded with reminders that the world is a violent, uncertain place and that women are frequently its victims.

Even women who live in relatively safe environments sometimes have little sense of control over their lives. They work nine-to-five jobs, keep house, raise children, and care for elderly parents. They feel pressure to excel at their jobs, have perfect children, be perfect wives. Housekeeper, caregiver, breadwinner, sex goddess. It all gets to be too much, especially when no one can promise us that everything will turn out all right in the end. That there will be enough money in the checkbook to pay the bills, that our Pap smear will come back negative, that our kids will stay away from drugs and our husbands will stay away from younger women. We yearn to cry out, "Please, God, make everything turn out all right!"

And in the romance novel, it does.

But how? The key to whether or not a romance novel gives me that satisfying sense of having some control over my life lies not so much with the personality of the heroine as with the type of hero the book depicts. While I can enjoy a book with a sensitive, caring, enlightened male standing steadfastly at the heroine's side as she works through her troubles, these books never give me the rush that tells me everything will be all right in my own life. Instead, I find comfort in books with dangerous heroes, cynical men who have grown jaded with life and love, men of action who not only refuse to stand by the heroine's side from the beginning of the book but who frequently make life more difficult for her.

This fictional "tough guy" hero is the sort of man I would never permit in my real life, so why is he so central to the empowerment fantasy? Do I have some secret sadomasochistic tendencies I'm not aware of? If I'm going to read romances—and I certainly am—why can't I enjoy books with the sort of sensitive, caring man I adore in real life? Why am I mentally salivating over an insensitive jerk suffering from an overdose of testosterone?

Book sales make it obvious that I am not the only woman in America who wants to read about this arrogant, domineering rogue—a man who, in real life, any intelligent woman would throw out the door in ten minutes flat. Virtually every historical romance writer who regularly appears on the *New York Times* bestseller list specializes in the tough guy hero: Catherine Coulter, Johanna Lindsey, Judith McNaught, Amanda Quick. Their success is not coincidental.

In the romance novel the domineering male becomes the catalyst that makes the empowerment fantasy work. The heroine isn't as big as he is; she isn't as strong, as old, as worldly; many times she isn't as well educated. Yet despite all these limitations she confronts him—

not with physical strength but with intelligence and courage. And what happens? She always wins! Guts and brains beat brawn every time. What a comforting fantasy this is for a frazzled, overburdened, anxiety-ridden reader.

Children deal with their fears of the real world by creating symbolic repositories of these fears—monsters who lurk in closets and bogeymen who hide under their beds. In a similar fashion the female romance reader finds her fears personified in the character of the virile and powerful rogue male, a character who serves not only as the hero of the novel but also, more subtly, as its villain, a potent symbol of all the obstacles life presents to women.

The scenes that make my heart beat faster are seldom the love scenes. Instead, my favorite scenes are always those in which the spunky heroine thrusts her chin up in the air and lays down the law to a towering, menacing, broad-shouldered male. She has no regard for her personal safety, the fact that he can flatten her with one sweep of his arm or crush her head between his hands as Rhett Butler threatens to do to Scarlett O'Hara—the fact that he can *kill* her if he wants to. She faces his rage with courage and, while he will almost certainly retaliate—sometimes with harsh, hurtful words, sometimes with aggressive lovemaking—she continues to defy him.

These scenes of confrontation become even more satisfying to me in books in which the hero actually has the power to kill the heroine without suffering any consequences himself. In the historical novels set during feudal periods, such as those of Johanna Lindsey and Jude Devereaux, he frequently has this option. He is lord of all he surveys with the power of life and death over his subjects. It would be quite easy for him to send this

feisty, bothersome, stubborn little critter who is caus-
ing him so much grief to her death or, at the very least,
into a lengthy and gruesome imprisonment. But he
never does this because she has ensnared him in an
emotional stranglehold that no amount of physical
strength or worldly power can break through. From the
moment they meet, he is a goner. All his muscle, wealth,
and authority are useless against her courage, intelligence, generosity, loyalty, and kindness.

I can only shake my head in bewilderment when I
hear the romance novel criticized for depicting women
as being submissive to domineering men. Are the critics reading the same books I am? What is the ultimate
fate of the most arrogant, domineering, ruthless macho
hero any romance writer can create? He is *tamed.*

By the end of the book, the heroine has brought him
under her control in a way women can seldom control
men in the real world. The heroine has managed to
change him from an emotionally frigid Neanderthal into
a sensitive, caring, nurturing human being. It is even
tempting to say that she has turned him into a woman,
and a case might be made for this were it not for the
fact that our hero still maintains his warrior qualities.
He is the mightiest of the mighty, the strongest of the
strong. But, because he has been tamed by our heroine,
because she exerts such a powerful emotional stranglehold over him, his almost superhuman physical strength
is now *hers to command.*

Shout hallelujah, Sister! No more fear of dark alleys!
No more worries about things that go bump in the
night! And, best of all, no more males who are unable
to understand the emotional needs of the female. The romance novel has—Abracadabra! Zap! Pow!—produced
two completely integrated human beings. It has pro-

duced the new male—strong and intensely physical, but possessing all the sensitive, nurturing qualities of the female. And it has produced a new female—a heroine who possesses all the softer qualities traditionally assigned to women but who has none of a woman's physical limitations because *his strength now belongs to her.*

Is the romance writer guilty of distorting reality? Of offering women a false view of their own power in the world? Guilty as charged, and thank God. Creating a fantasy world is one of the primary functions of all popular fiction. The mystery novel gives us a world of perfect justice, the western a world with no moral ambiguities. And the romance novel gives us two empowered and integrated human beings.

The romance novelist has an implicit contract with the reader who buys her book to portray life exactly as it is not. For the time that a reader is absorbed in a love story, she is not only safe from harm but empowered to rise above every limitation, every obstacle, every worry that confronts her. The heroine can be threatened, but by God that chin had better shoot up in the air pretty damn quick and those small fists had better start swinging.

Hold your ground, honey. Don't let him bully you. Go after him and don't give him an inch. Come on; do it for me, your loyal reader, because right now my feet hurt, the kids are fighting, and I've got cramps. Come on, honey. Just for a couple of hours, let me see a woman give as good as she gets.

Atta girl!

SUSAN ELIZABETH PHILLIPS

Susan Elizabeth Phillips is the author of two historical romances and four contemporary novels, including *Fancy Pants, Hot Shot,* and *Honey Moon.* Her books have been published by Dell and Pocket and have appeared on both the *New York Times* and *Publishers Weekly* bestseller lists. Her contemporary novels have been published internationally. She has received numerous awards from romance trade magazines and from organizations of fans and writers.

Ms. Phillips is a former high school teacher. She holds a degree in theater from Ohio University and did graduate work at the University of Iowa.

DAPHNE CLAIR

Sweet Subversions

George Eliot called them "silly novels by lady novelists." Charles Lamb condemned them as "these scanty intellectual viands of the whole female reading public." Germaine Greer said they "sanction drudgery, physical incompetence and prostitution." None of this censure had any noticeable effect on sales of romantic fiction.

Since the mediaeval troubadours brought to England tales of adventure, love, and derring-do, romance has never lost its appeal to popular taste. But around the seventeenth century, women's romance began to separate from men's romance. Men's romance now deals mainly with violence and death—in westerns, thrillers, and hard-core crime novels. And women's romance deals with the emotional life, relationships, and lasting love.

All men know that the female romantic novel is the product of and the fuel for women's fantasies. What they have not yet realised is that the fantasies are not about every woman's desire to be the willing sexual slave of some macho male. They are, and always have been, the subversive literature of sexual politics.

In 1688, when slavery was regarded as normal and necessary and the subjection of women as a state of affairs designed by God, Mrs. Aphra Behn published *Oroonoko; or, The History of the Royal Slave,* a liberationist tragedy of love, rebellion, and death that has a very good claim to be the first novel in the English language. Mrs. Behn advocated racial and sexual equality, and she made her living by her pen, the first woman in England to do so. She was regarded as no lady.

Simply by doing what they did, lady novelists were the vanguard of the feminist movement. And from the beginning, their writings subtly undermined the male establishment.

Love In Excess (1719) by Mrs. Eliza Haywood, the first woman editor of a women's magazine, and *The Reform'd Coquet* (Mary Davys, 1724) were early True Confessions written by ladies of doubtful reputation exposing the double standards of their day.

The Awful Warnings which abounded in such magazines as *Records of Love; or, Weekly Amusements for the Fair Sex* ("chiefly designed to promote a Love of Virtue in our Youth, by insinuating examples, and diverting passages") were highly necessary in a society in which seduction was a gentleman's legitimate leisure pastime and a girl who lost her virginity was almost inevitably doomed to the then real and common dangers of prostitution and disease, or death in childbirth.

Many of the women who wrote the stories, in an age when literary ladies were themselves regarded as only slightly better than whores, needed the money because their lovers had deserted them and their children.

The other theme of early romantic writing was Love Conquers All, or True Love Will Find a Way. Pure escapism, these stories offered a vision of freedom to women reared on such unpalatable advice as that given "to a daughter" by the Marquis of Halifax in *Ladies' New Year Gift* (1700). She should, the marquis instructed, patiently submit to the husband chosen for her, even if he were unfaithful, ill-humoured, miserly, or feeble-minded.

Men scoffed at stories of love and marriage even while they insisted that love and marriage and housekeeping were the proper province, and the only proper province, of women. They labeled the writers uneducated while they denied to women the educational opportunities they themselves enjoyed, and they called the readers ignorant and silly yet were offended by women who showed themselves to be anything else. There was a good deal of male thundering about the supposed frivolity of women's literature, and it was usual and expected for a female author to preface her work with a humble apology for daring to break into print and a plea for tolerance of the shortcomings of her sex. In literature as in life, the smouldering resentment of women at their lot, and their unshakeable conviction that at least in love their equality with men must be recognised, was hidden under a cloak of conventional submissiveness.

Miss Milner, the heroine of *A Simple Story* by Mrs. Inchbald (1791), dutifully obeyed her guardian Dorriforth's injunction to stay home more at nights, yet when Dorriforth became her fiancé she defied him in order to attend a masked ball of which he disapproved. Explaining the apparent inconsistency to her spinster companion she says, "As my guardian, I certainly did obey him; and I could obey him as a husband; but as a lover, I will not—if he will not submit to be my lover, I will not submit to be his wife—nor has he the affection I require in a husband."

At the end of the original two-volume version, Dorriforth admits at last to loving her "more than my life." "I cannot part from her," he cries and, falling upon his knees, implores her to marry him and "bear with all my infirmities."

Mrs. Inchbald's heroine insisted on the submission of the male to love, on his acknowledgement of her equality in their relationship, as the only way for a woman to survive the constraints of marriage, for once she was married a woman lost all rights to her money, her body, and even her children and her own name.

In a society where men had all the power, the only way for a woman to get a taste of it was to gain power over a man. Her sole weapon was her sexuality. Many women failed to use it to advantage, and this, the romantic writers told them, was because they married for the wrong reasons, thereby rendering themselves more powerless than ever. The only basis for equality was Mutual Love, with preferably rather more passion on his side than on hers.

In the late eighteenth century, Mrs. Ann Radcliffe changed the course of women's fiction and made the Gothic novel a peculiarly female genre. *The Mysteries of Udolpho* (1794) is the direct ancestor of the Brontës' novels, of du Maurier's *Rebecca*, Holt's *Mistress of Mellyn*, and every modern Gothic thriller.

At the beginning of the book Emily St. Aubert is living in a peaceful chateau set in an idyllic valley. Then her mother dies, her father becomes bankrupt, and he and Emily travel together through strange, exalted landscapes. On her father's sudden death, Emily is reluctantly fostered by an aunt who falls under the spell of Montoni, the bandit king, while Emily is in love with the rather limp but handsome Chevalier Valancourt.

Montoni carries the two women off to the Castle of Udolpho in the Apennines and locks the aunt in a tower, where she too dies. Emily remains imprisoned in the castle, a surrealistic architectural nightmare of vaulted passageways and mysterious chambers, haunted by ghastly apparitions and filled with distant echoes of bloodshed and lust.

In spite of a distressing tendency to swoon, Emily resolutely refuses to give up to Montoni the inheritance her aunt has left her and repulses his crony who invades her bedroom. She is acutely aware that the source of her greatest danger is also her only safeguard, and in the face of his proven predilection for vice of all descriptions she insists that Montoni has a duty to protect her.

Mrs. Radcliffe put into print women's deepest fears: the fear of being trapped and imprisoned in the house to which all women were supposed to confine their lives; the fear of male sexuality, male power, and male duplicity; and, not least, the fear of losing their own identity.

Montoni is a potent male symbol and a memorable literary creation. Intrepid Emily escapes him and after more adventures discovers she is the daughter of a marchioness and heiress to vast estates. Montoni is ultimately punished for his crimes, and Emily finally marries Valancourt, returning to an ordered life and domestic harmony with a nicely tame husband.

The several themes used by Mrs. Radcliffe still echo strongly in category romance. Heroines commonly are orphaned, come into a small inheritance, travel to foreign parts, and are employed—sometimes even kidnapped—by the dark, ruthless owners of large, isolated mansions. They often spend a chapter or two "finding themselves" or establishing their sense of identity, frequently assert their independence in the face of masculine assumptions of authority, and nearly always feel under threat emotionally if not physically from the dominant male in the story. But in one way or another, the heroine emerges victorious, enriched and with enhanced social status.

In the nineteenth century and after, a major subtheme of virtually all successful love stories—including those of Jane Austen, the Brontës, and their lesser imitators and literary heiresses—was the acquiring of money and of power. The heroes of romantic novels of this era generally have both.

Male critics of Jane Austen's works prefer to present them as satires. But female readers recognise her books as romances, concerned with the very serious business of husband hunting. *Pride and Prejudice,* its theme the subjugation of the rich, proud Darcy by the poor, proud Elizabeth Bennet, is a feminine favourite.

Darcy is described, in the first sentence in which he appears, as having "ten thousand [pounds] a year." Elizabeth naturally doesn't marry him for his money, but for the "respect, esteem and gratitude" she comes to feel for him after he uses his wealth and power to save her family from disrepute. Darcy's first, ungracious and grudging proposal was unsatisfactory in Elizabeth's eyes, but in his second he declares himself "properly humbled" and acknowledges that she has "shewed me how insufficient were all my pretensions to please a woman worthy of being pleased." Elizabeth now graciously accepts his suit, looking forward with unabashed delight to the time when she can enjoy "all the comforts and elegance" of his large estate—and his ten thousand a year.

* * *

And then came the Brontës. Emily and Charlotte Brontë gave a central place in their fervid, darkly romantic imaginings to what deep down all women knew, the thing that is buried in Ann Radcliffe's fiction. What women most loved, and most feared, was that dangerous, fascinating creature, Man.

In her towering novel *Wuthering Heights,* Emily Brontë fused the characters of hero and villain in the bitter, Byronic figure whose literary descendants still stalk glowering through the pages of many modern romances—the archetype Heathcliff.

Heathcliff is undoubtedly a Nasty Man. Only Emily Brontë's genius could retain a degree of reader sympathy for a brute who hangs his wife's lapdog before her eyes when eloping with her and mentally and physically maltreats her after marriage. But it is love for his darling, wayward Cathy that drives Heathcliff to all kinds of beastly behaviour toward her relatives. It is the memory of Cathy, seen in the eyes of her daughter, which makes him relinquish his magnificent vengeance. And when at last he gives up his wicked ways, Cathy's wraith returns to comfort but finally to kill him.

Female readers would agree with Cathy that the boorish Heathcliff was hardly husband material until he returned from his mysterious wanderings transformed by the acquisition of equally mysterious wealth. Wealth gave him power and polish—and attraction—although his basic instincts remained the same. It was Cathy's tragedy that meantime she had settled for marriage to a middle-class weakling.

Emily's sister Charlotte was shocked at the blunt portrayals of depravity in *Wuthering Heights.* Her own Mr. Rochester in *Jane Eyre* is less relentlessly horrid than Heathcliff, but he too is depraved, and something of a bully as well—unkind to children, impatient with old women, and sarcastic with young governesses.

Small, poor, and plain, Jane alone stands up to him, and when he cruelly teases her with his apparent intention to marry the wealthy beauty Blanche Ingram, Jane proclaims herself his equal in a famous, passionate speech.

Rochester tries to trap the innocent teenage Jane into a bigamous marriage, and when his deception is discovered does his utmost to seduce her and set her up as his mistress. Spurning his illicit proposition, Jane leaves him, discovers long-lost relatives, takes a job, and comes into a small inheritance. But in the end she acquires status and wealth through marriage to Rochester. For when he is at last free to wed her—although maimed and blind—she returns to his side.

Like her creation Jane Eyre, Miss Brontë was poor, plain, and frail, and put upon by the men in her life. But she took sweet revenge in her books and had her heroes shot, blinded, and drowned, while the heroines suffered steadfastly and retained their courage, their integrity, and their virtue.

Although Heathcliff maintains a tenacious hold on the popular perception, he is not the only prototype of the romantic male. In 1912, Jean Webster's *Daddy-Long-Legs* gave new life to Mrs. Inchbald's guardian-hero. Daddy-Long-Legs heroes (with traces of Mr. Rochester), lofty mentors many years the heroine's senior, were popular in early Mills & Boon romances. Eighteen-year-old child-brides, rescued from poverty and suitably grateful and biddable, in a year or two grow into ardent, determined women who claim equality with their now besotted husbands, as did Miss Milner and Jane Eyre.

Belying their outwardly pliant natures, the heroines of pre-1960s category romances exhibit—sometimes quite openly—a core of pure steel. They manipulate their men with a skill that is all the more impressive for being entirely unconscious. They chasten the chauvinists, reform the rakes, and marry the millionaires. Nothing can withstand the Love of a Good Woman.

Mary Burchell's gentle, motherly, tremulous Vicki, *Wife To Christopher* (1937), has promised to divorce her husband-of-convenience if ever his happiness should require it. But when he wants to marry the unspeakable Marie Renard, Vicki rejects his increasingly irate demands for his freedom, telling him firmly that he is merely infatuated and she knows what is best for him.

Christopher makes himself thoroughly unpleasant to poor Vicki, who fights back with infuriating feminine logic and patience until he comes inevitably to realise she is right. In the last chapter he is a pale, desperate, trembling wreck with no pride left, "big and sullen and scared . . . in the terror of wondering if she would tell him to go away . . . and was suddenly on his knees, clinging to her . . ."

It is ever so, in romance. The ultimate outcome is the powerful, successful man's recognition that his life and happiness depend on the love of a powerful and very special woman. The thrill is in the contest and the chase, in the complicated advance-and-retreat by which the strong-minded heroine, while appearing to be hunted and ill-used, finally turns the tables on and lovingly entraps the hunter.

Spanish grandees and Italian counts invariably begin by being impossibly arrogant and end abashed and bewildered, admitting that their own submissive womenfolk bore them to tears. Only an independent, liberated

English miss will satisfy their tempestuous Latin desire. Handsome young corporation heads cease giving their beautiful secretaries curt orders and confess that they cannot concentrate on adding to their considerable wealth unless the secretary consents immediately to becoming a wife. Lordly Amazon expedition leaders eat their disparaging words about women scientists after the heroine displays a capacity for courage, competence, and cool in the face of snakes, scorpions, poisoned darts, and male scorn. The subsequent proposal may be delivered through gritted teeth, but he knows that he can't live without her.

If his passion is laced with anger and resentment, she doesn't mind that. It's no fun having a tame tiger about the house if it's toothless. And taming tigers is what it's all about.

By the 1970s, heroines no longer hid their inner strength but gloried in it. Strong heroines demanded ever stronger and more dangerous heroes, and the struggle was more openly for what used to be called mastery.

In Mary Wibberley's *The Taming of Tamsin* (Mills & Boon, 1978), when Blaise Torrance enters the story he "exuded a kind of power and strength rarely seen" and displays every conventional sign of male superiority. By page 169 "Tamsin felt almost sorry for Blaise. He looked like a man who didn't know what was happening." And on the last page he whimpers, "Don't ever leave me again. Don't frighten me."

But in victory the romantic heroine is magnanimous, and once he has admitted his crying need of her, the hero is allowed to crawl back to a modicum of self-respect, because all she ever wanted, really, was his acknowledgement of her worth.

* * *

Even the wildest dreams of women have their roots in reality. The stories may be rose coloured and the characters and their emotional reactions rather larger than life, but the problems of romantic heroines of today, like those of previous centuries, are problems daily faced by many readers, which they will seldom find dealt with in men's popular fiction or "serious" literature.

Romance offers fantasies that address the sometimes intimate concerns of women in a male world. After the First World War maimed a generation of men, Edith Maude Hull gave their women *The Sheik* (1921), a healthy, uncomplicated male with straightforward lusts who took the initiative in no uncertain terms and didn't ask that his partner be strong, compassionate, and understanding. Half a century later, in the very teeth of women's liberation, Kathleen Woodiwiss's *The Flame and the Flower* and Rosemary Rogers's *Sweet Savage Love* generated a flood of immensely successful rape-romances that enraged feminists, created guilt in many avid readers, and were cited as perpetuating the notion that women really do like being forced. (We might assume then that men, major consumers of thrillers, westerns, and detective fiction, enjoy being beaten up, tortured, shot, stabbed, dragged by galloping horses, and thrown out of moving vehicles.)

"Sweet savage romances" feature spirited heroines fighting tooth and nail but constantly being ravished—in both senses of the word—by handsome, virile, often angry men who finally repent of their sins and settle down to wedded bliss. Taking to its extreme the strong-man-brought-low-by-strong-woman plot, and openly expressing what Mrs. Radcliffe's dark passageways and bloodied swords could only symbolise, these "bodice rippers" enable women whose greatest terror is rape to face it safely between the pages of a book, which they know quite clearly has no resemblance to real life but where they can contain and control the experience. This may well be a perfectly valid way of dealing with fear—within the context of a genre which men proudly declare they never read.

Writers who eschewed the rape romance were nevertheless emboldened by Rogers, Woodiwiss, and others, and in the mid-1970s there was a flowering of sexuality in women's fiction as writers of both historical and contemporary romances explored with a new freedom the heady possibilities of erotic writing *for women.* A few men, nudged by their women, began reading romances to find out how women would really like to be made love to. Some, shocked by female writers venturing into traditionally male territory, decided that the books were pornographic, a label nicely designed to stop "decent women" from reading them.

Other themes examined from a feminine perspective under the covers of romance include career/marriage conflicts, single motherhood, clinical depression, divorce, adultery, impotence, infertility, incest, child abuse, wife beating, tug-of-love custody battles, gang rape, widowhood, workaholic behaviour, alcoholism, prostitution, drug addiction, war and its aftermath, and recently surrogate motherhood, anorexia, and mastectomy.

Women now, including women in romantic fiction, may well be powerful and rich in their own right. There is less emphasis on the hero's income and social position and more on the heroine's profession, a trend discernible in the 1940s and 1950s, years before the new wave of feminism gathered momentum.

Instead of ballerinas, opera singers, or doctors, not to mention secretaries, nurses, and housekeepers, contemporary heroines are likely to be pilots, racing drivers, engineers, or corporate executives. They may be in their thirties or forties, older than most heroines of twenty years ago, while the typical hero is often younger and less sure of himself than formerly. Yet the classic elements of romance still hold the imagination of vast numbers of readers. Beneath the faultlessly cut suit or designer jeans of many a civilised, seemingly liberal modern hero lurks the untamed savage, Heathcliff. But no matter how he struggles and fumes, in the end he is tamed and domesticated by a woman's gentle strength.

In the 1980s, American romances began to challenge the British tradition. A new adjective appeared in editorial guidelines and on book jacket blurbs as "feisty" heroines did battle with their men and eventually conquered them. And American editors—strongminded career women with perhaps an uneasy feeling that the macho hero with whom they spent their working lives was politically incorrect—began insisting on sensitivity, humour, understanding, and patience in the romantic man. Not content with claiming the right of equality with men, they now boldly demanded that men should, dammit, be more like women—the ultimate subversion.

Veteran romance readers know that these qualities were always present in romantic heroes. It just took a special kind of woman to uncover them, and they were perhaps revealed only to her—although animals, children, and old ladies might be specially privileged, a fact that the heroine will have noted.

But American writers obliged by producing the Tom Selleck nice-guy jogging hero, big and handsome, funny, warm, and vulnerable. Instead of sexual antagonism they used style, wit, emotional warmth, and sometimes explicit, tender, and sensual love scenes to hold reader interest. These books may bore or baffle male literary critics, but their readers keep coming back for more. One of the truisms of literature is that all fiction is built around some form of conflict, classically expressed as "man versus man, man versus his environment, man versus himself." Having already added to the canon "woman versus man," some romance writers are quietly challenging that ancient literary law, in effect subverting accepted male-defined notions of the nature of fiction itself.

The American soft-centered romance has taken its place alongside other popular variations on the romance theme. But so many readers objected to the bland, politically correct hero that now the editorial cry is "Come back, Heathcliff!" Sweet, sensitive, New Age men who may be wonderful husbands in real life don't provide enough challenge and excitement for the fantasies of strong, confident, successful 1990s women. The classic intractable fictional hero still enthralls the female imagination.

Romantic heroes are arrogant autocrats and macho males, not because women are masochists but for the same reason that 007's enemies possess all that unlikely technology. Victory over a weak and ineffectual adversary is not worth much. But when a woman has a big, tough, powerful male on his knees and begging her to marry him, that's a trophy worth having!

A smoking .45 and six corpses at his feet is a male fantasy. A woman will settle for one live hero at hers. And if she places a dainty foot upon his neck, it is only to invite him to kiss it.

Portions of this essay appeared in the Christchurch (New Zealand) *Star*, 25 June 1990.

DAPHNE CLAIR (LAUREY BRIGHT, CLAIRE LOREL)

Daphne Clair de Jong is a third generation New Zealander whose first published story was written when she was fifteen. Her short stories have won literary prizes at home and abroad, including New Zealand's premier Katherine Mansfield Award (1981). In 1986 she won the PEN NZ Lilian Ida Smith Award for nonfiction and was runner-up in the Cambridge Toyota National Short Story Competition. Her stories have appeared in collections and anthologies including *Women's Work* (Oxford University Press, NZ, 1985) and *New Women's Fiction* (New Women's Press, NZ, 1991). She is currently completing a historical novel with a New Zealand background.

Ms. de Jong has published about forty series romances with Mills & Boon/Harlequin (as Daphne Clair) and Silhouette (as Laurey Bright), and two Regency romances with Fawcett/Ballantine as Claire Lorel.

She is a qualified librarian who has worked in public and school libraries.

DOREEN OWENS MALEK

Mad, Bad, and Dangerous to Know

The Hero as Challenge

When I was asked to write this essay about the appeal of romance novels, I thought back to what the books offered me years ago, when I was just a reader and had never written one. It is the same thing my readers tell me that the books offer them now: escape, certainly, but escape into a very particular fantasy of which they never tire.

In the late fall of 1978, when I was in my third year of law school, I landed in the hospital as an emergency case with an F.U.O. (fever of unknown origin). My mother was dying of cancer, my final exams were coming up in three weeks, and the grades for the courses I was teaching were due (hence the F.U.O.). I was hooked up to intravenous tubes, forbidden to exercise or work, and, worst of all, had nothing to read.

The patient who had occupied the bed before me left behind a stack of Harlequin romances. I knew about them, of course, had seen them around, but I was a doctoral candidate and very impressed with myself. If I were going to read anything in my nonexistent leisure time, it would be Proust or Stendahl or at the very least *Huckleberry Finn.*

The first book I picked up was Anne Mather's *Leopard in the Snow.* Its hero is a racing car driver: tough, courageous, cynical—very macho. At the beginning of the book he is a jaded recluse, disgusted with the world (and women) but by the end the heroine is the center of his life. The leopard was tamed.

And I was hooked. Nothing could be further from chemotherapy and Landlord-Tenant Law than this. Escapism, you bet, and just what I needed. The fantasy was there. I couldn't have articulated it then, in fact I hadn't even identified it, but I felt its presence and it drew me more powerfully with each successive romance that I read. By the time I left the hospital I had gone through all the books I had.

I then wanted more of the Harlequins. But I was afflicted with that well-known two-symptom disease of most law students characterized by no time and no money. I could not linger in bookstores or lavish cash on a personal library. I grabbed the books secondhand when I could, which wasn't often because I was working long hours at a men's prison writing appeals for convicted felons. Happily, however, the second-year student working with me saw me carrying a romance one day and said, "Oh, do you like those? Me, too. Got any more at home?"

After this we sought out other romance lovers at school and established an informal exchange system. We harried students did not analyze why we loved romances—remember, no time—we just knew that we did. The stories were often slight, the heroines could be very silly, and the people in the Harlequins talked funny (Brit funny—they were always driving "minis" or being struck by "lorries" or going "on holiday" in the Cotswolds—where?). None of it mattered; we didn't care. We traded books like baseball cards and sped off to the next class. We needed distraction from the grinding routine of briefs and patriarchical judges and unreasonable professors and the type of clients we were dealing with every day.

The books provided this distraction, and we devoured them as we prepared Constitutional arguments on the rights of women and stumped for the ratification of the ERA. It never occurred to us that anyone might see a conflict between our behavior and the behavior of the people in the stories we liked. One was reality, the other was entertainment, and nobody was confused. We cherished the fantasy for what it was, an intoxicating illusion, then packed up our papers and hurried off to court.

So what is the fantasy? Simply this: a strong, dominant, aggressive male brought to the point of surrender by a woman.

Why does this particular fantasy hold so much appeal for us? Because it dramatizes, colorfully and dramatically, a battle of the sexes in which the woman always wins. Women are weaker physically, perennially behind in civil rights, always playing catch-up ball with men. This type of fiction offers a scenario in which a woman inevitably emerges victorious. The hero may swear and stomp and deny and resist and fight like hell and give the heroine a terrible time (my favorite type of story, in fact), but in the end he capitulates because he simply must have her.

This is exactly why the tough hero, the subject of so much debate, is absolutely fundamental in such a romance, the tougher the better. Winning against a wimp is no triumph, but bringing Linda Howard's John Rafferty *(Heartbreaker)* or Elizabeth Lowell's Cord Elliott *(Summer Games)* or Kristin James's Cutter *(Cutter's Lady)* to heel? Now there's a victory. We may want a caring, sensitive, modern man in our lives, but we want a swaggering, rough-hewn, mythic man in our books. He provides the best foil; the more obdurate the hero, the sweeter the triumph when the heroine brings him to his knees. We can put up with inadequate plotting; dithering, petulant, even childish heroines; and numerous other flaws as long as the essential element is there—the fantasy, the compelling relationship with an indomitable hero who becomes so fascinated by and enthralled with the heroine that by the end of the book he will do anything to possess her.

For years I've been subjected to a barrage of criticism regarding my fondness for romances. First it was, "My God, you're a law student and you read this stuff?" Then it was, "My God, you're a lawyer and you *write* this stuff?" I'm always amused when such critics accuse romances of being unrealistic—talk about missing the point! Of course they're unrealistic, that's *why* we like them. Anybody who wants realism can find it in the nonfiction section of the bookstore or on the news in the latest travails of the beleaguered people of Bangladesh. And when "feminists" attack romances and call them the new opiate of the female underclass, pabulum fed to the proles to keep them content with their sorry lot, I think of Sharon's mother.

Sharon was a friend of mine in law school, and her mother was a widowed teacher who raised her three daughters from preschool age alone. These women are today a doctor, a lawyer, and a civil engineer. They all entered male-dominated fields and in them became self-sufficient, self-supporting, and successful. Their mother's favorite author was Kathleen Woodiwiss.

Can anyone seriously argue that Sharon's mother was a member of some subjugated and helpless group or had raised her children to take their place in it? To her the heroine of *Shanna* was not a role model, she was a diversion, a diversion which this woman sorely needed in order to endure a hard life of bringing up three children by herself on a teacher's salary. In Shanna's world there are no pediatrician's bills, absent husbands, or hostile teenagers, and Shanna always triumphs in the end. And the reason these books are a diversion, the reason they are entertaining and amusing and fun, is that in them we get to play out our favorite fantasy: the juicy, seductive conflict with a sensational man which we know in advance the woman can never lose.

By the word "fantasy" of course I don't mean that the location must be the planet Aros and the heroine the valedictorian of the space academy. Anyone familiar with these stories knows that they have a framework of reality, like the contemporary romances in which the heroine may work in an office and the hero may own a construction company, or the historicals set in a particular period. My recently completed historical, *The Highwayman*, is set in Elizabethan England and I did my best to get the period details right, but the relationship between the hero and the heroine is pure fantasy. The backdrop is there, and it once existed, but the scene being played out in the foreground involves kidnappings and rebels living in the woods like Robin Hood and a heroine dressed up as a boy: all those things for which we surrender our hard-earned coin because we know they never happened but enjoy imagining that they could.

By the time I attended the 1986 Romance Writers of America conference in Minneapolis I had published several different types of books, but romance remained my first love. When talking to the other authors, I realized that everyone was discussing a two-part TV movie that had recently been broadcast called *Harem*. The author of the teleplay, Karol Ann Hoeffner, had written a romance novel for television, and the conference attendees universally recognized this. The story had all the elements, but what brought us special joy was the ending of the film, which as I have already pointed out is so critical to the romance. Let me describe it.

Our heroine (Nancy Travis), after maný highly improbable foreign adventures, has fallen hard for our rebel hero (the sublime Art Malik, terrific as usual). He has already proven himself dedicated to a noble cause (the big one, freedom), brave beyond recklessness and dashing beyond words. But he's a very tough character (his first act was to sell her into slavery to obtain the release of his men) and is fighting his conquest by the heroine fiercely. Captivated by her intelligence, her integrity, and the courage which she displayed even while she was physically powerless, as well as by her beauty, he has already been vanquished emotionally but still won't admit that he loves her. Our heroine, resigned, is about to board the train to go home with her boring fiancé (ubiquitous Julian Sands in a thankless role) when they hear the sound of gunshots. Out of the desert gallops our hero, flowing white robe streaming behind him, yelling and firing his rifle in the air. As the passengers stand transfixed he rides straight to the feet of our heroine, impales her with his burning dark gaze and says, "What do I have to do to make you stay?"

Well, you know the rest. She dumps the boyfriend,

climbs onto the horse with gorgeous, and rides off over the dunes.

Every romance reader watching this has just shouted "Yes!" and thrown a victory salute into the air. Why is this ending so satisfying? Not only because love has triumphed, but because he has capitulated and she has *won*. He's willing, finally and at the very last minute and after much resistance, to do anything to keep her with him. This is the ultimate fantasy, the quintessential escapist fare. Karol Ann Hoeffner knows what every romance writer and reader also know: unreality is the name of the game, and in this unreal world everything must come out right in the end.

The summer of 1989 was a low point in my life. During the previous six months my father, a beloved aunt, and my first baby had died, all under miserable circumstances. I was undergoing gruesome tests for various rare conditions and had lost even the desire to work, which is really ground zero. My doctors were issuing prescriptions for "mood elevators" and tranquilizers; they couldn't seem to decide whether I should be jacked up or knocked down. Instinctively reaching for my own cure, I junked the pills and got out the books.

Out of the cellar came all the old Candlelights and Silhouettes and Joves, along with the Laurie McBains and Emma Drummonds. I became the best customer of the several swap shops in my area and spent all of my time reading, which was a distinct improvement over spending all of it screaming. And gradually, slowly, I read less and thought about working more. The escape the books provided really helped me, and is it any wonder? In a reality where a pitiless, random fate had buffeted me almost beyond endurance, the books offered a universe in which fate is under control, because in the end it is always the heroine's friend and always gives her exactly what she wants.

When I am outlining a new story, an experience which for me holds all the terror and frustration of driving in Los Angeles (a traffic jam in a desert) or New York (a traffic jam in hell), I am never worried about providing role models. I leave this to Mother Teresa and Marie Curie and Mary McLeod Bethune, because I am fully aware that my readers aren't looking for idols in my books. They're looking for the fantasy—they say so. They say so over and over again in their letters, but more importantly, they say so with their money. The bestsellers, the books that zoom onto the various lists that tabulate such things, always feature the toughest, most incorrigible heroes, a pitched battle for much of the story, and triumphant heroines at the end. Examine them and see if you can disagree.

This has traditionally been true, even in the days when books were not identified as "romances." I don't know how old I was when I first read *Jane Eyre*, but I was young enough to think that the heroine's name was pronounced "eerie" and to need a dictionary as a companion volume to decode all the unfamiliar words. Riveted by the developing relationship between testy, caustic Rochester and feisty, implacable Jane, I was undeterred by the plummy dialogue and by Charlotte Brontë addressing me intermittently as "Reader." I didn't care, it didn't matter, because even then I knew that the fantasy was there.

And what about Rhett Butler, for heaven's sake, that consummate rogue, the sine qua non of romantic heroes? I do know how old I was when I discovered *Gone with the Wind*. I was twelve and in the seventh grade; I remember because I was caught reading it when I was supposed to be contemplating the error of my ways in isolated detention. For this further infraction I was given a day's suspension (during which I finished GWTW, which gives you an idea of the kind of school it was. If you were caught smoking, you were shot. Not surprisingly, most of my classmates were heavily into escapist fiction). Why did Rhett capture my attention, as he had already captured the world's? Because the fantasy was there. And don't quibble about the ending—Scarlett has already won several times in the book, most notably when Rhett asked her to marry him after trailing her all over the old South. I was always sure they would get together again about a week after Rhett walked off into the mist, anyway. After all, tomorrow *is* another day.

I could go on, ad infinitum, boring you with more examples, but the point has been made. This is the type of story we like, and why shouldn't we have it? It's labeled fiction, nobody thinks it's real, and it harms no one.

My husband, ever the logical lawyer, is fond of saying that if he once behaved the way the heroes do in my books I'd serve him with separation papers the same day. And he's right—because we, for better or worse, are inhabiting reality. In reality, the water pump breaks and the water line freezes and your five-year-old develops strep throat on Christmas Eve. In reality, your client is a jerk and the judge hates your face and your opposition is a pinstriped hockey jock from Harvard. Is it so shocking that we might want to escape reality for a few hours with a book? During this time we can have a glorious adventure with Shanna or Scarlett or whatever name Spunky Susie is wearing this week, taking on the bitchin'est, kickin'est, mucho macho guy on the block.

The kids, the cramps, the mortgage, and the job will all be there when we put the book down and come back. So critics be damned; bring on the Cords and Dirks and Bricks, the Lord Ravenscrofts and Ravensdales and Ravensbrooks. I'll be waiting. We'll *all* be waiting.

DOREEN OWENS MALEK

Doreen Owens Malek has published fourteen series romances with Silhouette and a contemporary romance with Warner. She has also published *Clash by Night,* a World War II novel, with Worldwide, and historical romances with Harlequin. Future titles include *The Highwayman* with HarperCollins and *The Panther and the Pearl* with Leisure Books.

Ms. Malek's awards include the Romance Writers of America Golden Medallion for *Crystal Unicorn* and a *Romantic Times* magazine award for *Danger Zone.* Six of her books, including *Desperado, Roughneck,* and *A Marriage of Convenience,* have appeared on the Waldenbooks Romance bestseller list.

Ms. Malek was a high school English teacher and reading specialist before becoming an attorney. She has worked in the legal field in Springfield, Massachusetts and Hartford, Connecticut.

ROBYN DONALD

Mean, Moody, and Magnificent

The Hero in Romance Literature

The strong, domineering hero of the romance novel has long been the subject of criticism. What critics don't realize is that it is the hero's task in the book to present a suitable challenge to the heroine. His strength is a measure of her power. For it is she who must conquer him.

Every good romance heroine must have a hero who is worthy of her. And in most cases he is a mean, moody, magnificent creature with a curling lip and mocking eyes and an arrogant air of self-assurance—until he meets the heroine.

She is the only person who can make him forget his natural courtesy, lose his rigidly-controlled temper; when he is faced with her determination to do what *she* feels is right for her, he reacts in ways he knows to be despicable or at the very least unworthy of his principles. The spirited, somewhat bewildered heroine senses that she is the only person who has such a powerful effect on him, just as he is the only man who can make her reassess the foundations on which she has built her life until then. She is able to read the small signals that tell her he is trustworthy, even though his hardness and antagonism may repel her at first. And the signs of his helpless response to her are intercepted by feminine intuition. He may say he dislikes her, he may even act as though she is as treacherous as he believes her to be, but arrogant and overbearing, even brutal though he may be, he never acts in a way which makes her truly fear for her physical safety. A hero is kind to animals, to children, and to little old ladies.

But even before she sees this, at some purely instinctive level, the heroine knows she can trust him. However, she also knows that the initial attraction is powerful but almost entirely sexual. She understands that there is much more to love than physical attraction, and she is not going to bestow her future on the hero until he, too, realizes this.

It takes him some time. Heroes are men who admit to being difficult to live with, who demand extremely high standards in every aspect of their lives, who are natural, effortless leaders, strong men, men with prestige and intelligence, whose faults are likely to be manifestations of strength and power. He is the master of his life; he is in control. Whether his sphere of influence is the boardroom or the mountains, the sea or the stage, the hero dominates it with his personality, his intelligence, and his quick, hard-honed grasp of every situation. A hero can seem arrogant and short-tempered, ruthless, tough, even cruel—he can be quite unlovable at first.

Why do women enjoy reading about such men, whose only redeeming feature at first seems to be that they fall violently and completely in love with the heroine? In most cases readers are happily married to men who bear no resemblance to this pattern of masculinity.

It has nothing to do with some masochistic need to be mastered. Indeed, in a romance the heroine is never mastered; she conquers the hero.

Until very recently in our historic past, strong, successful, powerful men had the greatest prospects of fathering children who survived. If a woman formed a close bond with a man who was sensible, competent and quickwitted, one high up in the family or tribal pecking order, a man with the ability to provide food and protection for her and any children she might have, the chances of her children surviving were greater than those of a woman whose mate was inefficient.

Such a man needed certain attributes, attributes which surface in romantic heroes. He needed to be agile and physically well developed, as well as intelligent, able to sum up a situation swiftly and to react instantly. Looks are not important, although the human hunger for beauty has given rise to many handsome heroes. For the safety of the woman and her children, he had to be able to temper his strength and toughness with compassion and care. Ruthlessness and a possessive streak might also be useful, and this man would need as well to have the ability to love his woman, deeply, powerfully, faithfully.

To be the only, much-loved mate of such a man would have distinct survival value for both the woman and her children. A romantic hero may have a character that is less than perfect, but he must be shown to have the capacity to love and a basic human sense of responsibility and compassion. He is an authoritative figure; he takes charge in an emergency with the knowledge that what he is doing is the best that can be done under those particular circumstances. He is successful.

This powerful man, confident in his standing and his

masculinity, sure of himself; competent and trustworthy, discovers during the course of the romance that without the heroine he is no longer able to enjoy his life. *He needs her.* He may kidnap her, he may force her into marriage, he may coax or intimidate her into his bed, but eventually he learns that her physical presence, even her sexual surrender, is not enough. He needs her to come willingly to him, not as a slave to be conquered but as an equal in all respects. He learns, usually with some pain, that to be truly happy himself he has to make her happy.

As she learns to trust him, he must learn to trust her, to understand that he can reveal to her his hidden core of vulnerability. Slowly he comes to realize that the only thing that will satisfy him is her admission of love for him, her equal commitment to a shared life. Equal partners in every way, they will live out their life together.

It is this which is the powerful and seductive fantasy at the core of all romance fiction.

ROBYN DONALD

Robyn Donald is a pseudonym for Robyn Kingston. She has written over thirty-two romance novels, which have all been published by Mills & Boon/Harlequin. With over 15 million copies of her novels sold, she is one of their bestselling writers. *Summer Storm* appeared on the Waldenbooks Romance bestseller list. Her novels have been translated into as many as twenty different languages including Magyar. Ms. Kingston makes her home in New Zealand.

ANNE STUART

Legends of Seductive Elegance

I write the vampire myth: legends of seductive elegance, of beauty that could kill as well as redeem, stories both eerie and erotic. It's a fantasy that has always spoken to me directly, fulfilling emotional needs I've never bothered to define. It's a fantasy that speaks to a great many other women, if I can judge by what they've told me.

At the heart of the vampire myth is a demon lover who is both elegant and deadly, a creature whose savagery is all the more shocking when taken with his seductive beauty and style.

Dracula, with his pale skin and deft, delicate hands, wears white tie and tails. He knows the things to say and do in polite society, he knows how to lure a willing female to her doom. Even Death himself, in the romantic play of the 1920s, *Death Takes a Holiday,* was urbane and sophisticated, passing himself off as an Italian peer.

There is a place in romance, in my own fantasies, for the laconic cowboy, for the over-civilized power broker, for the gentle prince and the burned-out spy. They all have their appeal, their merits, their stories to tell.

But the vampire myth strikes deep in my soul.

Deep in my heart I want more than just a man. I want a fallen angel, someone who would rather reign in hell than serve in heaven, a creature of light and darkness, good and evil, love and hate. A creature of life and death.

The threat that kind of hero offers is essential to his appeal. The cover copy of my first book, a 1974 gothic, described the hero as "a dangerous but compelling man who was either trying to murder her—or seduce her. Or perhaps both." My reaction at the time was a resounding "yes!"

This is a different fantasy from the rape fantasy or the "you Tarzan—me Jane fantasy" or the "come here, woman" fantasy, all of which have their place, politically correct or not. This is no truck driver with ready fists. This is a man of murderous elegance, Cary Grant in *Notorious,* a man who knows the rules and ignores them. A man whose sense of honor and decency is almost nonexistent. A man with a dark midnight of the soul. The heroine can either bring light into the darkness or risk suffocating in the blackness of his all-encompassing despair.

The heroine's attraction to the hero is never in doubt. While she represents sanity and love, she is willing to relinquish family, friends, career, life itself in giving herself to the vampire hero. She is willing to give up everything, to become an outcast. The fire of his appeal is worth the risk of conflagration.

The stakes are much more interesting when there's something at stake beyond happy-ever-after. The bond between heroine and hero is more than romantic, more than social. It is a spiritual, intellectual, sexual bond of the soul, one that doesn't end with till death do us part. It is a bond that surpasses death and honor and the laws of man and nature. It takes on an entity of its own, greater than the sum of its parts.

I need something beyond comfort and safety in my fantasy world. In real life I'm sensible enough to search for just those pragmatic things. A life of delight and despair is, in reality, too exhausting.

But in fantasy I want it all. I want a man larger than life, a man capable of killing, of destroying everything when the demons inside him take control. And I want a heroine to save him from those demons, leading him into light.

For some readers the fantasy is too threatening. The connection between death and sexuality can be disturbing to some readers, those who prefer sunlit meadows to moonlit caverns. For a vampire legend to work, its humor must be black, its pacing rapid, its mood intense. There is no room for gentle couplings beneath a starry sky. Each coming together must have the resonance of eternity.

For others, for those who love my books and for me, the threat is what makes it work. The dark hero is what makes it worth the risk. Balanced on the edge of a precipice of emotions, the heroine learns it's worth the plunge to find the kind of soul-shattering love that can come from a man balanced on his own edge. The heroine must be very sure, very brave, very worthy. And if her triumph at the end is death in his arms, then we know that at least they have eternity.

Fortunately in romances there are no unhappy endings. The vampire/beast/phantom/demon in the hero doesn't win. The schizophrenic battle waged within him is won—with the love of the heroine and with the hero's humanizing ability to love.

But the demon isn't vanquished. He is always there,

a threat, a promise lurking beneath the elegance of a partially reformed hero, because his darkness is the other half of the heroine's light. And it is from that yin-yang, that perfect match, that eternity comes into play, changing a simple meeting of minds and bodies into something that transcends time and space.

We all look for that transcendence, each in our own way, through our own fantasies. For me, the threat of death at the hands of love is the most potent fantasy of all. Only if you're prepared to risk everything can you gain everything. And only in fantasy can women have it all.

ANNE STUART

Anne Stuart has published more than thirty-seven books in a variety of genres including series romance, historical romance, romantic-suspense and suspense. Her publishers have included Dell, Ballantine, Doubleday, Fawcett, Harlequin, Silhouette and Avon. *Night of the Phantom* is the title of one of her recent releases. Her novel of suspense, *Seen and not Heard,* was published by Pocket Books.

Ms. Stuart's novels have appeared on the Waldenbooks Romance bestseller list, and she has won numerous awards from romance trade magazines and from organizations of fans and writers. Her book *Banish Misfortune* won the Romance Writers of America Golden Medallion award for best single-title release.

ELIZABETH LOWELL

Love Conquers All

The Warrior Hero and the Affirmation of Love

At first glance, reader mail seems to address the question of why women continue to read romances in the face of society's relentless disapproval. One after another, readers write to me and say: *Your romances are so intense. Such tough, powerful men. I just love them!*

That's gratifying to hear, but it begs the question of why women read romances. After all, if formidable men were all that women wanted, there is a plethora of fierce, forceful males in mystery, science fiction, historical sagas, thrillers, and male adventure novels. (I know, because I've written and published all but the latter.)

What, then, in addition to formidable men, attracts women to romances? Is it the intensity of the emotional experience?

Again, if an intense emotional involvement with the story were the key ingredient for which romance readers yearn, there is an abundance of intense emotion to be found in mystery, science fiction, historical saga, thrillers, and particularly horror novels.

Compelling, formidable men. Intense emotions. Neither is unique to the romance genre. What else do romances have that make them unique among genres of fiction and uniquely compelling to women of many religions, races, and cultures?

Reader mail does not answer the question. It would be surprising if it did. At bottom, it is not up to the readers to explore why they love romance novels; readers, after all, are not professionals. Authors are, especially successful authors. If you consult the best-selling romance novels, you quickly find a common thread that is unique to the genre: only in romances is an enduring, constructive bond—love—between a man and a woman celebrated.

That is the key. That is what makes romances unique and uniquely powerful in their appeal.

Other styles of fiction deal at length with hate, murder, greed, lust, treachery, brutality, pettiness, vicious sexuality, violence, and unspeakable human degradation. If love appears in these novels it is in a minor role, a comet burning across the dark night of the soul leaving greater darkness in its wake.

In romance novels, and in romance novels alone, love between a man and a woman is affirmed as an immensely powerful *constructive* force in human life. As subtle and universally pervasive as gravity, love touches everything, enhances everything it touches, and binds men and women into an extraordinary sharing that both transcends the everyday world and gives people strength to cope with life's daily demands.

Does that mean all you need for a compelling romance novel sure to be prized by readers is sweetness, light, and love, love, love?

It is more complex than that. Even John Milton's

prodigious talent was strained when he tried to create a compelling depiction of *Paradise Regained.* Dante Alighieri did no better; the section of *The Divine Comedy* called "Inferno" is part of our popular culture, but "Paridiso" is known only to English majors. Sweetness and light is wonderful in life and deadly in drama.

How then does one make a romance—a celebration of creation rather than destruction, good rather than evil, love rather than hate—intense and compelling to readers? Given the readers' expectation of a constructive resolution of the central conflict (also known as the much-maligned happy ending), from what source comes the vital dramatic tension of the romance novel?

The same place it comes from in a mystery; that is, from the process of resolution rather than from the resolution itself. The reader knows when she or he picks up a mystery that the ending is guaranteed; the crime will be solved. That is why people read mysteries. The certainty of resolution attracts rather than deters mystery readers. I suspect that mystery fans are people who believe that human problems can be solved by intelligence and logic (and judicious head cracking). They seek out fiction that speaks to their belief in the power of rational, disciplined human beings to solve life's problems.

If the destination is not in doubt, the intensity the reader seeks must inevitably come from the journey itself. In mysteries, the reader wants to see how close the crime can come to defeating the protagonist's attempts to unravel it. The crime must be a worthy adversary, testing the power of human logic to defeat chaos, and the resolution must be believable within the confines of the novel. Only then will the reader have the satisfaction of reaffirming that human intelligence can triumph over the boggling illogic of life.

It is a comforting thought, rather like that of the power of love to heal and ultimately to transcend the random cruelties of life. (Oddly enough, critics rarely speak of neurotic readers, mindless escapism, or formulas when mysteries are mentioned, but protagonist meets crime, protagonist is baffled by crime, protagonist solves crime is the requirement of mystery fiction.)

Romance readers, like mystery readers, take their intensity from the journey itself rather than from uncertainty as to the ultimate outcome. Romance readers know that love fails in real life; they want the believable possibility of love's failure in their fiction. They want love to be tested to the limits of its power to heal and transcend. They want the power of creation to battle with the power of destruction. They want to balance on the razor edge of the abyss of despair. And then they want to soar in triumph, their belief in love's constructive power affirmed by a battle hard fought and well won.

Pleasing such readers is not an easy task for the author. With heaven foreordained, how can the struggle appear anything more than pro forma?

Enter the fierce, formidable male, the tougher and stronger the better. Nothing sharpens your appreciation of heaven like a guided tour of hell.

It is the formidable hero who puts the heroine at risk of losing her future and herself to a man who does not believe in love. It is the bleak, powerful hero who puts love's transforming power to the ultimate test. After all, there is little emotional danger to a heroine who loves a saint. The reader has no sense of risk, of loving and losing, of the possibility of creation overcome by destruction, when the hero in question is a good man from his genial smile to the penny loafers on his feet. But when the man is older, stronger, unsmiling, capable of violence, a warrior seasoned in hell . . .

The possibilities for psychic and even physical danger to the heroine are manifest and vivid with this type of man. The woman who loves a formidable man, hardened in life's unloving crucible, will test love's healing power in a very intense way. The closer love comes to failure, the sweeter the affirmation when love triumphs.

That, and not culturally induced feminine masochism, is why fierce, almost savage men abound in the most popular romance novels. That is why romance heroes often are not only capable of violence, they are specifically trained for it. They are warriors, the paradigm of the formidable male.

The warrior-as-hero has one other important qualification: he is not a psychotic brute intent on destroying everything slower, weaker, or less vicious than he. The warrior-as-hero accepts the discipline of the larger society. He has made the fundamental choice to use his skills to protect others rather than merely for his own enrichment. He has voted on the side of construction rather than destruction. He is an honorable man.

Despite this underlying, often tacit assurance of the hero's basic decency, there is always a tension between the lethal capabilities of the hero and the relative physical helplessness of the heroine. Obviously he could take her whenever he wanted, just as he could brutalize children, bully weaker men, and in general be a destructive, unappealing brute.

The classic romance warrior-heroes *do not enjoy destruction.* Ultimately they use their strength, their intelligence, and their discipline to defend rather than exploit those who are weaker than they. At core, they are decent men. The heroine senses this, just as she senses that the warrior's profession often has the effect of excluding him from the same society he protects. It is the beginning of her understanding that this formidable man might be capable of love. For example:

> Raine looked up at Cord, sensed his male power and need, his body trained for death and his eyes hungry for life. Tears gathered in her eyes, blurring Cord's outline, leaving only the crystal intensity of his gaze.
> "You've risked so much," she whispered, "you've given so much, and you've never known the warm world you make possible for others. You could die without knowing that world, like a sentry barred from the very fire he protects."[1]

Classic romance heroines are neither vapid Pollyannas nor closet masochists. Very early in the novel, the heroine both senses and triggers the need for love that lies within the hero. She also senses that success—mutual love—is possible. Not guaranteed. Perhaps not even probable. But possible. That possibility is enough to make the heroine risk her own happiness, her own *self* in a journey that could well end in heartbreak. Another example:

> He wanted to ask where her softness and strength had come from, to know if he could ever love as she did, with sweetness and fire and courage. But he couldn't ask that. So he asked the only question he could, and Angel heard the other question beneath it, the one Hawk couldn't ask.

"Are these wild raspberries?" asked Hawk.

"No. They're like a house cat that has gone feral," Angel said. "Created and bred by man and then abandoned. Most things treated like that wither and die. Some survive . . . and in the right season the strongest survivors bear a sweet, wild fruit that is the most beautiful thing on earth. Like you, Hawk."[2]

Yet, even with insight into the hero's potential for love, love is not an easy thing to achieve, especially with a warrior. Warriors believe in loyalty, honor, strength, and death. Life and love are rather more slippery propositions. Though a part of the best warriors hungers for life, for warmth, for love and children and laughter, that very yearning is viewed as a weakness in a world where weakness is an invitation to death.

A man who views love as a potentially lethal weakness is not likely to give in easily, even when he wants and needs love very much. The following scene is an example. The hero, Nevada, was formerly a commando sent to help the Afghani tribesmen covertly against the Soviets. Eden, the heroine, does not know that part of Nevada's training including going from sleep into full fighting mode if he is awakened in an unexpected way. At the moment, they are in an isolated mountain cabin, where she has taken him after a riding accident. He is in the grip of a feverish sleep:

Eden knelt at Nevada's side. She put her hand on his forehead to gauge his temperature.

The world exploded.

Within the space of two seconds Eden was jerked over Nevada's body, thrown on her back and stretched helplessly beneath his far greater weight while a hot steel band closed around her throat. In the wavering firelight Nevada's eyes were those of a trapped cougar, luminous with fire, bottomless with shadow, inhuman.

"*Nevada . . .*" Eden whispered, all she could say, for the room was spinning away.

Instantly the pressure vanished. Eden felt the harsh shudder that went through Nevada's body before he rolled aside, releasing her from his weight. She shivered with the cold of the cabin floor biting into her flesh, and with another, deeper cold, the winter chill that lay at the center of Nevada's soul.

"Next time you want to wake me up, just call my name. Whatever you do, don't touch me. Ever."

Nevada's voice was as remote as his eyes had been.

"That's the problem, isn't it?" Eden asked after a moment, her voice husky.

"What?"

"Touching. You haven't had enough of it. Not the caring kind, the warm kind, the gentle kind."

"Warmth is rare and temporary. Cruelty and pain aren't. A survivor hones his reflexes accordingly. I'm a survivor, Eden. Don't ever forget it. If you catch me off guard I could hurt you badly and never even mean to."[3]

It will take an unusual heroine to get past this warrior's defenses long enough to show him that love strengthens rather than weakens a man. Eden knows this, as her inner dialogue shows:

Nevada won't be an easy man to love. He's a winter man, shut down deep inside, waiting for a spring that hasn't come.

On the heels of Eden's thought came another, a realization as unflinching as winter itself.

Don't kid yourself. You're going into this with your eyes wide open or you're not going at all. Nevada isn't waiting for spring. He probably doesn't even believe spring exists. That's quite a difference.

It's a difference that could break my heart.[4]

The risk of love's defeat is real. The characters know it, the author knows it, and the readers certainly know it. In fact, they demand it. The readers want the heroine to be put through merry hell, for only in that way is the strength of love ultimately affirmed. Nor is the heroine alone in her travails. The hero as well must have his time of realization, when he understands what his refusal to love has cost.

The course of true love must run as rough as a mountain cascade, for it is the steepness of the grade that brings out the seething power and beauty hidden within still water.

Romance readers know that cruelty, defeat, and despair are a part of life. But romance readers also know that there is more to life than mean, narrow, ugly, nasty, brutish, and short. They believe in the power of love between a man and a woman, love that heals and enhances life. They want to read fiction that speaks to this deeply held belief.

Inevitably, they read romances. For this, they are routinely ridiculed in a manner that would be considered repellent were it applied to race, religion, or sexual preference. Women keep reading romances anyway, for these novels allow them to affirm and to celebrate their deeply held beliefs about woman, man, and love.

I share with my readers an abiding belief in the beauty and constructive power of love between a man and a woman. Giving flesh and blood, face and voice to that belief is one of the greatest pleasures of my varied career as an author.

NOTES
1. Elizabeth Lowell, *Summer Games,* published by Avon.
2. Elizabeth Lowell, *A Woman Without Lies,* published by Avon.
3. Elizabeth Lowell, *Warrior,* Silhouette Books, April 1991.
4. Ibid.

ANN MAXWELL (ELIZABETH LOWELL)
Writing as Ann Maxwell, Ann began her career in 1975 with a science fiction novel, *Change.* Since then, seven of her nine science fiction novels have been recommended for the Science Fiction Writers of America Nebula Award; *A Dead God Dancing* was nominated for the American Book Award. Her science fiction was published by TOR, Popular Library, Signet/NAL, and Avon.

In 1976 Ann and her husband Evan (as A. E. Maxwell) collaborated with a Norwegian hunter and photographer, Ivar Ruud, on *The Year Long Day,* a nonfiction work that was condensed in *Reader's Digest* and published in four foreign editions and three book club editions. In 1985 the first A. E. Maxwell crime novel, *Just Another Day in Paradise,* featuring a couple called Fiddler and Fiora, was published by Doubleday. The second in the series, *The Frog and the Scorpion,* received a creative writing award from the University of California. The fourth book in the series, *Just Enough Light to Kill,* was named by *Time* magazine as one of the best crime novels of 1988. The series has continued to enjoy critical success. The seventh title, *The King of Nothing,* was published by Villard (a division of Random House) in July 1992. Ann and Evan are presently writing *Come Hangman! Come Vultures!* which will be the eighth in the Fiddler and Fiora series.

In June 1992 Ann and Evan (writing as Ann Maxwell) had a suspense novel, *The Diamond Tiger,* published by HarperPaperbacks. They are presently researching *The Secret Sisters,* another suspense novel for HarperPaperbacks. Writing under the name Lowell Charters, Evan and Ann recently completed *Thunderheart,* a novelization of a movie by the same name. It was published by Avon in April 1992.

Beginning in 1982 Ann began publishing romances under the name Elizabeth Lowell. Under that name she wrote twenty-one series romances for Silhouette, many of which have appeared on the Waldenbooks Romance bestseller list. Two of her latest three, *Warrior* and *Outlaw,* placed in the number one position. She also wrote a historical romance and one book of romantic suspense, *Tell Me No Lies,* for Harlequin. The latter was reissued in August 1992.

At present Ann is writing historical romances for

Avon. Her first, *Only His,* spent almost two months on the B. Dalton mass market bestseller list. *Only Mine,* published early in 1992, appeared in the top ten on both the Waldenbooks and B. Dalton bestseller lists.

MARY JO PUTNEY

Welcome to the Dark Side

What is the appeal of romance? That's an unfortunate question for those who like simple answers, for genre romance is not monolithic but diverse and ever-changing.

While women read romance for many reasons, a vital ingredient is the romantic spirit of optimism, a belief that life is improvable, that the glass is half full not half empty. The subliminal message is that one's life can get better, a belief that is one of the bedrocks of American society. Of course romance readers are aware that not all situations will improve, but a good romance offers a pleasurable respite from the vexations of everyday life.

Romance is fantasy, and like all genre fiction it reflects the world as we would like to see it, with crime punished, justice triumphant, goodness rewarded, and love conquering all. Characters are larger than life, with stronger passions, blacker faults, and brighter virtues. However, while all romances are fantasy, the tone varies greatly from pure escapism to stories that contain much more realistic elements.

Historical romances have an advantage in creating fantasy worlds because our view of the past is selective; many readers have a fondness for the Middle Ages, but the fantasy is of brave knights and lovely damsels, not of serfs laboring in the fields. Similarly, the popular English Regency setting has produced enough fictional lords to fill Yankee Stadium, and the fictional Wild West teems with hard-eyed gunslingers and dashing gamblers. As with all fantasy, even the most outrageous premise can work if it is developed in a logical fashion, with convincing details.

Kathe Robin, the historical reviewer for *Romantic Times* magazine, divides romances into two types: those that come from the light side and those that come from the dark side. Light romance evokes laughter and sweetness, while dark romance works with more intense emotions.

Which brings me to one of the principal reasons that people read romance: for the emotion. While the best books of any genre create vivid characters and memorable relationships, romance is the only genre that by definition centers on feelings and relationships rather than on plot or abstract concepts. The most popular romance writers are those who have the ability to evoke strong emotional responses and make readers care about the characters. An emotional writer can transcend technical writing flaws, but a technically correct romance without emotion will be forgotten almost as soon as the book cover closes.

While intense emotion is one factor that distinguishes light romance from dark, an even more significant factor is the hero. As most thoughtful romance aficionadas know, the hero is the most crucial character in a romance, the linchpin who holds the story together. This is a key difference between romance and what is usually defined as women's fiction, where the heroine and her progress through life are the focus of the story.

A romance can survive a bland or even a bitchy heroine, but it cannot succeed with a weak hero. Not only must he be a man the reader can fall in love with, but he also sets the tone of the book. (My thanks to author Jo Ann Wendt, who first brought this point to my attention.) A light, laughing hero will create a light, playful book, while a dangerous hero is at the heart of most dark romances.

Often the dark hero is obsessed with the heroine, driven by a primitive passion to possess her in every sense of the word. An aura of potential—and sometimes actual—violence hovers over such books. As Jayne Ann Krentz says, the male protagonist of a romance is often both hero and villain, and the heroine's task and triumph is to civilize him, to turn him from a marauder into a worthy mate whose formidable strength will be channeled into protecting his woman and his cubs (sorry—his children).

The wounded hero is a subcategory of dark hero. He is emotionally and/or physically damaged and, like an injured lion, he is dangerous, for he is still powerful and in his agony he may lash out at those around him. Loving him makes the heroine vulnerable, yet only she, with her love, compassion, and female strength, can save him from his demons.

The theme of the man who is "saved by the love of a good woman" is common in both life and romance. In reality savior complexes are dangerous because they encourage women to stay with abusive mates, but that is another story, one that belongs in "women's fiction" rather than "romance." What matters in a romantic context is that healing the wounded hero is a fantasy of incredible potency. Not only does it appeal to the nurturing instinct, but a woman who can heal an injured man has great power. She is a success in a very female way, for she has saved the Alpha male, the leader of the pack, and can now share in his strength.

It is much rarer to see the heroine saved by the love of a good man. It *is* possible to write a romance where the heroine is more tortured than the hero, and I have done so, but it is more difficult and probably less "romantic." To make a tortured-heroine romance successful, the hero must be a compelling figure in his own right, not a passive foil for the heroine's problems. While he is supportive and understanding, he must have a role beyond drying her tears or the story fails as romance.

My own particular form of dark romance is not for everyone, for it occupies a shadowy corner of the romantic turf where fantasy meets gritty reality. Alcoholism, incest, sexual abuse, rape, dyslexia, epilepsy, and various other physical and psychological injuries—I've written about them all.

Welcome to the dark side.

Other writers have often said to me, "I can't believe your editor let you get away with that." While admittedly I have been lucky in my editor, I think that virtually any topic can be handled if it is done properly, with a romantic sensibility. (It helps that I write historical novels, where the setting puts some distance between the reader and the issue.)

Alcoholism is a topic most romance editors would reject out of hand. However, I was irritated by the fact that in historical books heavy-drinking men are often seen as dashing, with no negative consequences, so my book *The Rake and the Reformer* had an alcoholic hero.

Anyone familiar with addiction and twelve-step programs can read the book and see the hero, Reggie, go through the stages of denial, attempted reform and failure, and the final breakdown—the shattering of the will—that must be experienced before there can be a chance for spiritual and physical regeneration.

However, no one buys a romance to get a temperance tract. The heart of a romance *must* be the relationship, so Reggie the Rake was matched by Alys the Reformer, who was compassionate without indulging in codependent behavior. As in all good romances, the main characters encourage each other to heal and grow; as Alys supports Reggie through his ordeal, Reggie in turn helps Alys to face her past and rebuild her damaged self-esteem.

Since many Americans—probably a majority—have had painful experiences with alcoholics, *The Rake and the Reformer* struck deep chords in readers. Not only did the book win several awards and become a word-of-mouth bestseller, but the fan mail demonstrated how profoundly the story touched people. One newly recovering alcoholic said simply, "You'll never know what that book meant to me."

Another recovering alcoholic wrote at greater length: "Reggie is the most realistic alcoholic I've ever read. He was not a bum, or a continuous drunk, or any of the other stereotypes I've seen before. He was a person with a serious problem, yet he was strong enough to overcome it. Though my battle was fought over a longer period of time, you captured the despair, the strength, that moment of serene, inner determination so vividly, I almost seemed to go through it all again. . . . Alys's tender support [was] so perfect for him that I cried buckets. And the hope! Lord almighty, lady, I haven't had a story evoke so much emotion since I read my very first romance novel."

While such readers clearly respond to the realism, it is essential to maintain the balance between realism and romantic fantasy. Hence I torture my characters in a variety of ways. The initial trauma may have taken place in the past, with the story focusing on overcoming the effects, or the wounded character may be secondary rather than one of the central lovers.

That is how I treated epilepsy in my historical romance, *Dearly Beloved*. The heroine's young son has a moderate degree of epilepsy, but the condition is presented as a regrettable nuisance rather than a disaster. Geoffrey is a nice little boy, matter-of-fact about his condition, and not above faking a seizure to try to get his own way. In short, he is very human, a child with a problem but also a reasonable expectation of having a fulfilling life, and he generated a number of intensely-felt fan letters.

However, epilepsy was a minor problem compared to the trauma suffered by the hero, Gervase, who was seduced by his amoral mother when he was thirteen. As a guilt-ridden and angry young man, it was hardly surprising that he responded to a shot-gun marriage by forcibly claiming his "marital rights" from his new bride, whom he wrongly assumed had been a party to the scheme. The result was a rape as rape really is: an ugly, violent crime that was damned near unforgivable, with nothing erotic about it.

The heart of the story takes place years later as the protagonists struggle to overcome the disastrous beginning to their marriage and forge a healthy, loving relationship. As always in my books, the hero and heroine help each other grow: the heroine, Diana, uses her warmth and compassion to help Gervase recover from the abuse of his past, while Gervase's bleak, hard-won honesty forces Diana to confront her own hidden motives.

This is hardly escapist fare, but readers responded positively; in fact, members of the Romance Writers of America nominated *Dearly Beloved* as one of the top ten books of the roughly fifteen hundred romances published in 1990 (as *The Rake and the Reformer* was so nominated in 1989). One reader wrote, "Your characters are so real and have real problems. The way they deal with the problems is what makes your books special."

Dark stories that deal with intense emotions can provide catharsis and insight into painful problems. The point is not the injury; disease-of-the-week would be dreary. What matters, and what readers respond to, is the healing, for it is profoundly moving to read about an incest victim who manages to transcend the pain, to become stronger in the mended places, who can forgive the past, even if she or he can never entirely forget it.

The fantasy framework makes it possible to confront emotions too painful to deal with in a more realistic context. No matter how gravely damaged the protagonists are, they find emotional salvation through love. Ideally, romantic love is not presented as a panacea; instead, it is a catalyst that helps the hero and heroine become whole enough to give and accept love.

While no one lives a full life without experiencing pain, romance readers are not the sort to relish a lifetime of misery. The events in most romances usually take place over a relatively short time span, almost always less than a year. (Even in "lost-love" romances where there has been betrayal and years of separation, the real-time action of the story is generally only a matter of weeks.) During the course of the book the hero and heroine come to terms with their problems, and by the end the future looks bright, for even the darkest romances are leavened by liberal doses of warmth, hope, and tenderness.

What makes dark romances feasible is the safety net; no matter how threatening the situation or how wounded the body and spirit, the reader of a genre romance knows that all of the issues will be satisfactorily dealt with by the end.

Ironically, the happy ending that makes dark romances possible is the source of many criticisms of the genre. "Serious" literature is usually a gloomy affair, a well-crafted rendition of the numerous ways that life can go wrong.

Yet gloom and doom are not inherently more realistic than happiness, for all lives cycle through ups and downs, good times and bad. A romance simply chooses to focus on the magic moment when two people are falling in love and the world is a place of infinite possibilities.

MARY JO PUTNEY

Mary Jo Putney has published twelve historical romances, including *Silk and Shadows, Silk and Secrets,* and *Veils of Silk,* all with Penguin/NAL. Her novels appear on the B. Dalton's, Waldenbooks and Reader's Market bestseller lists. She has received numerous awards from romance trade magazines and from organizations of fans and writers, among them the Romance Writers of America RITA award for *The Rake and the*

Reformer. Romantic Times magazine honored her *Dearly Beloved* as the best Regency historical of the year. She has been a finalist in the Romance Writers of America Golden Choice contest for best romance of the year.

Ms. Putney has degrees in English literature and industrial design from Syracuse University. Before she began her writing career she had her own business in the field of graphic design and held a position as art editor for a British magazine.

JAYNE ANN KRENTZ

Trying to Tame the Romance

Critics and Correctness

Don't think that there hasn't been a lot of pressure exerted to make romance writers and romance fiction more politically correct. During the past few years, even as romance novels have commanded a spectacular share of the publishing market there has been an unrelenting effort to change them.

Much of this effort was exerted by a wave of young editors fresh out of East Coast colleges who arrived in New York to take up their first positions in publishing. (The editing of romance novels has traditionally been viewed as an entry-level job in the industry.) These young women (and most of them were women) didn't read romances themselves and so didn't understand why they appealed to readers. But they did understand that romance novels are held in contempt or at the very least considered politically incorrect by scholars and intellectuals and even by much of the publishing hierarchy which makes billions of dollars from them. And so they set about trying to make romances respectable. They looked for new authors who shared their views of what a respectable romance should be and they tried to change the books being written by the established, successful authors they inherited.

The first target of these reforming editors was what has come to be known in the trade as the alpha male. These males are the tough, hard-edged, tormented heroes that are at the heart of the vast majority of bestselling romance novels. These are the heroes who made Harlequin famous. These are the heroes who carry off the heroines in historical romances. These are the heroes feminist critics despise.

What is it with those of us who write romance? We are intelligent women. We're flexible. We learn fast. Surely those who sought to lead us in the paths of politically correct romance writing ought to have succeeded in their goal of straightening us out by now. Why did we dig in our heels and resist the effort to turn our hard-edged, dangerous heroes into sensitive, right-thinking modern males?

We did it for the same reason a mystery writer sticks to the outcast hero, the same reason a western writer clings to the paladin figure. We did it because, in the romance genre, the alpha male is the one that works best in the fantasy.

And the reason he works so well is because in a romance the hero must play two roles. He is not only the hero, he is also the villain.

To understand what the romance novel is, it is important to understand first what it is not. A romance novel plot does not focus on women coping with contemporary social problems and issues. It does not focus on the importance of female bonding. It does not focus on adventure. A romance novel may incorporate any or all of these elements in its plot, but they are never the primary focus of the story. In a romance novel, the relationship between the hero and the heroine *is* the plot. It is the primary focus of the story, just as solving the crime is the primary focus of a mystery.

Given that conflict is a requirement of all good fiction, especially good genre fiction, and given that the conflict must arise out of the primary focus of the story, it is understandable that in a romance novel conflict must exist between the hero and heroine.

The hero in a romance is the most important challenge the heroine must face and conquer. The hero is her real problem in the book, not whatever trendy issue or daring adventure is also going on in the subplot. In some way, shape, or form, in some manner either real or perceived on the heroine's part, the hero must be a source of emotional and, yes, sometimes physical risk. He must present a genuine threat.

The hero must be part villain or else he won't be much of a challenge for a strong woman. The heroine must put herself at risk with him if the story is to achieve the level of excitement and the particular sense of danger that only a classic romance can provide.

And the flat truth is that you don't get much of a challenge for a heroine from a sensitive, understanding, right-thinking "modern" man who is part therapist, part best friend, and thoroughly tamed from the start. You don't get much of a challenge for her from a neurotic wimp or a good-natured gentleman-saint who never reveals a core of steel.

And it is that core of steel at the center of a good romance hero that makes it all worth while.

Any woman who, as a little girl, indulged herself in books featuring other little girls taming wild stallions knows instinctively what makes a romance novel work.

Those much-loved tales of brave young women taming and gentling magnificent, potentially dangerous beasts are the childhood version of the adult romance novel. The thrill and satisfaction of teaching that powerful male creature to respond only to your touch, of linking with him in a bond that transcends the physical, of communicating with him in a manner that goes beyond mere speech—that thrill is deeply satisfying. It is every bit as powerful as the satisfaction readers get from seeing the outcast hero solve the crime and mete out justice in a good mystery. But to get the thrill, you have to take a few risks. The hard-boiled detective must go down a few dark, dangerous alleys and the romance heroine must face a man who is a genuine challenge.

The second target of those who attempted to change romance novels was another familiar convention in the books: the aggressive seduction of the heroine by the hero. Most of the time this seduction is portrayed as intense and unrelentingly sensual; occasionally it is so forceful that it has been mislabeled rape by critics. Either way it is a convention that is universally condemned by those who sit in judgment on the romance novel. It is not politically correct for a woman to fantasize about being aggressively seduced.

It is odd that the romance genre is singled out for this particular criticism, because the aggressive seduction of the protagonist is an extremely common convention in most of the other genres. Mysteries, a field notable for its plethora of both male writers and male protagonists, routinely use this approach to dealing with sex.[1] Many hard-boiled private-eye heroes get themselves seduced by their female clients or suspects in the course of the story. The seducing client or suspect is frequently portrayed as potentially threatening and as having a strong aura of aggressive sexuality, a description that nicely fits romance heroes. In mysteries the private eye very seldom initiates the seduction and, indeed, often appears surprisingly passive about the whole thing. Some put up a token resistance not unlike that put up by the heroines of some romance novels. This aggressive seduction of hard-boiled private investigators could conceivably be mislabeled as rape, but critics rarely even bother to mention it.

Aggressive seduction of the protagonist occurs in other genres as well. The male heroes of thrillers and men's action-adventure novels[2] are frequently swept off their feet and into bed by mysterious, exotic, powerful women. It is only when the tables are turned as they are in the romance genre, when the female protagonist is seduced by a mysterious, exotic, powerful male, that critics become alarmed.

It would seem to be more accurate and more honest simply to acknowledge that the fantasy of being aggressively seduced within the safe, controlled environment of a work of fiction is a popular one shared by men and women alike. And why not? It's very pleasant to enter into a fantasy where one is the treasure rather than the treasure hunter.

It is interesting to note that in the romance novel this fantasy often takes on a complex and fascinating twist. Through the use of male viewpoint, a technique often employed either directly or indirectly, the reader is allowed to experience the seduction from the hero's point of view as well as that of the heroine. The reader gets to enjoy the fantasy of being *simultaneously* the one who seduces and the one who is seduced.

This twist on the basic seduction fantasy is not a simple matter of the writer structuring the scene so that the reader switches back and forth between viewpoints. It cannot be summed up or explained by saying that the seduction is witnessed first through the heroine's eyes and then through those of the hero. In a really good romance, the experience for the reader is that of being in both the heroine's mind and the hero's *at the same time*. The reader knows what each character is feeling, what each is sensing, how each is being affected. She is also profoundly aware of the transcendent quality of the experience, of how it will alter the course of both the hero's and the heroine's life. The whole thing is incredibly complex, exciting, and difficult to describe. I suspect it is almost unique to the romance novel.

Perhaps it is this indefinable richness of the seduction fantasy that makes romance novels so threatening to critics of the genre. But just because one does not have the vocabulary fully to explain the experience does not mean it is a negative one. It does not even make it politically incorrect. The truth is that women who read romance novels never describe themselves as feeling threatened by the fantasy of being seduced, just as men who read hard-boiled detective fiction never appear to feel threatened by the sexually aggressive client or suspect.

The third target of those who sought to make romance novels respectable was the convention of the heroine's virginity. There is no denying that the most popular romances, both contemporary and historical, frequently feature heroines who are virgins. This fact is readily acknowledged by writers such as myself, who have compared royalty statements with other writers. It is also substantiated by an examination of the best-seller lists.

This virginal quality has nothing to do with making the heroine a "trophy" for the hero. Nor is it used as a moral issue. It has everything to do with creating a metaphor for the qualities of female power, honor, generosity, and courage with which the heroine is imbued. Virginity has been the stuff of legends, of stories of kings and queens, bloody wars and patched-up alliances, territorial feuds and historical consequences since the dawn of time. There is a heroic quality about a woman's virginity that is truly powerful when used to its fullest potential in fiction.

There is also the underlying assumption in most romance novels that the heroine is smart enough to choose the right man. It is to this man that she gives the gift of her love and her virginity. Part of being the hero of such a romance novel means appreciating the gift of the heroine's virginity. *She* is never the same again. Perhaps even more important, *he* is never the same, either.

In a romance novel the heroine allows herself to be seduced not by just any male but by one particular male, a larger-than-life hero. She takes a risk, and at the end of the story it pays off. She has chosen the right man. She has tamed the magnificent wild stallion. She has awed and gentled him with the generous gift of herself. She has also forced him to acknowledge her power as a woman as well as the womanly honor she uses to control and channel that power.

Men represent to women one of the greatest sources of risk they will ever encounter in their lives. Taking risks and winning out against all odds is one of the great pleasures of fantasy. In a romance novel the heroines put everything on the line and they win. Virginity is symbolic of the high stakes involved.[3]

The fourth target of the reforming editors was the genre's frequent use of certain core stories. It has often been pointed out that there are only a handful of plots available to the mystery genre and only a few basic stories in western or science fiction or horror. This limitation on plot devices is not considered a sin in those genres, but for some reason critics view it as such in romance.

At the core of each of the genres lie a group of ancient myths unique to that genre. The most popular writers in those genres continually mine those ancient myths and legends for the elements that make their particular genre work. Westerns and mysteries incorporate the old chivalric tales. The horror genre relies on the gut-wrenching myths of the supernatural that have been around since the days when people lived in caves. Science fiction uses the myths of exploration and the fear of the "other" that have long fascinated an aggressive species bent on conquering new territory. At the heart of the romance novel lie the ancient myths that deal with the subject of male-female bonding.

Stories become myths because they embody values that are crucially important to the survival of the species. There is no subject more imperative to that survival than the creation of a successful pair bond. The romance novel captures the sense of importance and the sheer excitement of that elemental relationship as no other genre can.

Women, who have traditionally had the primary responsibility for making that bond work, have always responded to the basic myths and legends around which romance is built. I suspect they will continue to do so as long as the current method of reproduction is in use and as long as the family unit is the cornerstone of civilization.

Some of the basic myths and legends that animate the romance genre include the tale of Persephone (echoed in a thousand stories involving a woman being carried off by a mysterious, powerful male who is in turn enthralled and brought to his knees by her). Another popular one is the story of Beauty and the Beast (often portrayed in childhood tales of little girls taming large stallions and in adult stories of women taming dangerous men). Then there is the familiar battle of the sexes, or the Taming of the Shrew story. This one is especially piquant for women because in these tales the man is the one who, for once, is forced to find a way to make the relationship work.

There are other basic stories of romance, all of which have deep roots in ancient myths and legends. In the romance novel the elements of those myths and legends that speak most powerfully to women are preserved and retold.

Romance novels are tales of brave women taming dangerous men. They are stories that capture the excitement of that most mysterious of relationships, the one between a woman and a man. They are legends told to women by other women, and they are as powerful and as endlessly fascinating to women as the legends that lie at the heart of all the other genres.

The effort to make romance novels respectable has been a resounding failure. The books that exemplify the "new breed" of politically correct romances, the ones featuring sensitive, unaggressive heroes and sexually experienced, right-thinking heroines in "modern" stories dealing with trendy issues, have never become the most popular books in the genre.

Across the board, from series romance to single title release, it is the writers who have steadfastly resisted the efforts to reform the genre whose books consistently outsell all others. And the readers have demonstrated where their hearts are by routinely putting the romances that incorporate the classic elements on the bestseller lists.[4]

NOTES

1. The propensity of the heroes of mystery novels toward getting themselves aggressively seduced is readily seen in many of the books throughout the genre. From the novels of Raymond Chandler and Dashiell Hammett to the books written by such popular contemporary authors as Dick Francis, Loren D. Estleman, Scott Turow, and Andrew Vachss, it is almost always the woman who does the seducing.

2. In the quintessential men's action adventure series, *The Executioner,* the hero, Mack Bolan, is a man who is certainly aggressive when it comes to dealing out a violent kind of justice to the bad guys. But when it comes to women he is politely aloof, almost reluctant. It is the women in the stories who pursue and sometimes manage to seduce him, not vice versa.

3. I am indebted to romance writer Suzanne Simmons Guntrum for many of the ideas and much of the language I have used in this discussion of virginity.

4. An examination of any of the romance novels written by the following *New York Times* bestselling authors will prove this point: Judith McNaught, Sandra Brown, Johanna Lindsey, Catherine Coulter, Karen Robards, Julie Garwood, Amanda Quick. For more names, check the latest edition of the *New York Times* bestseller lists.

DOREEN OWENS MALEK

Loved I Not Honor More

The Virginal Heroine in Romance

Romance novels are criticized for all manner of things, and often those conventions most cherished by the readers are selected for the harshest censure. The virginal heroine is one of these conventions. In spite of virginity's fall from grace (so to speak), the virginal heroine has lost none of her popularity with readers. As I tried to address the question of why such heroines are so appealing, I recalled Sister Charles Eileen, who stimulated my own interest in the subject about twenty-five years ago when she introduced me to the Vestal Virgins.

Raised in a religion which has its own cult of the Virgin and taught from the age of five by nuns, I was probably set up for the Vestals from the start, but Sister Charles Eileen, my first-year Latin teacher, made certain that virginal heroines would have lifelong significance for me. A stern, dignified woman with the intellect of a Jesuit, she had the most essential quality of a great teacher: she was in love with her subject. And since a language can scarcely be separated from the people who speak it and whose culture it

communicates, she was really in love with the ancient
Romans.

After a couple of months in her class, so was I. Their
spectacular accomplishments, their stunning savagery,
even their imperious mode of expression (a grammati-
cal form devoted to direct address and imperatives!) enthralled me. I loved Cicero's essays, the maxims of
Marcus Aurelius, the narratives of Caesar's campaign
against that wily Celt, Vercingetorix. Roman politics
and warfare brought to mind their modern counter-
parts; I could fairly hear Cato thundering "Delenda est
Carthago!" at the end of each of his speeches. And Tac-
itus's tales of Boadicea, warrior queen of the Iceni who
led a rebellion against the Roman occupation of Britain
in the first century A.D., were especially spellbinding.
But best of all I loved reading about the Vestals.

The Vestal Virgins were a group of six women, selected from the finest Roman families, who gave their
lives to the service of the goddess Vesta, keeper of the
hearth. They dedicated themselves to tending the sacred
flame burning in the circular temple where Vesta was
worshiped. Because the Romans believed that the burning of this perpetual fire was a protection against national calamities, maintaining it was a sacred trust. The
Vestals remained virgins all their lives; if they broke
their vow of chastity they were put to death. In the early
days of the Republic, before Rome decayed into empire,
this worship of Vesta was taken very seriously. The
Vestals were cultural icons, heroically sacrificing the
feminine fulfillment of home and family for a higher service to the community. They were deeply respected but
also most strictly observed, so that a lapse in morality
meant swift and certain retribution.

To my fevered fourteen-year-old mind, the dramatic

possibilities of this scenario were endless. I immediately began daydreaming about a forbidden romance between a beautiful Vestal and a handsome centurion who are drawn to each other during the public ceremonies of Vestalia in June. Their passion would be irresistible, their scandalous liaison discovered, and just as she was about to be executed he would ride to the rescue (à la Lancelot saving Guinevere from the stake—I was also reading Tennyson at the time). As they say in Hollywood, what a concept. And as I got older and learned more about female virgins as the personification of purity and perfection, I began to realize that my fascination was shared by many and that the virginal heroine was the stuff of myth.

Thomas Bulfinch and Edith Hamilton kept me awake nights in high school with their anthologies of ancient myths, and the best stories, the ones that lingered in my mind with almost biblical impact, always concerned unique, virginal women who behaved with extraordinary courage and passion and style. Diana the huntress, twin sister of Apollo and goddess of the moon; Ariadne, who led Theseus through the labyrinth; Atalanta, who could beat any man in a footrace; Daphne, who was pursued by Apollo and turned into a laurel tree for refusing his advances; Cassandra, also pursued by Apollo and cursed with the gift of unheeded prophecy for refusing his advances (Apollo was never a good loser): the list of virginal heroines from Greek and Roman mythology is long and impressive. And our own Anglo-Saxon tradition follows suit: from Robin Hood's Maid Marian and Tennyson's Elaine, "the lily maid of Astolat," to the women of Jane Austen and Longfellow's Evangeline, we mirror the ancients in our admiration for and fascination with the virginal heroine.

Why are virgins so special? Over time I have con-
cluded that it is because they are *in* the world but not
completely of it, since they have not participated in that
essential earthbound activity which transforms a girl
into a woman. When "primitive" peoples wanted a perfect gift for their gods, when they were seeking the most
worthy offering to hurl from a cliff or stab through the
heart or throw into the mouth of a volcano, they didn't
select the most popular mother of five in the village or
the most beautiful courtesan. They selected a virgin as
the gift most acceptable to their gods, and she offered
her life to serve the common good by petitioning or pro-
pitiating those gods: for a bountiful harvest, surcease of
plague, victory over an enemy, or whatever else the
community desired. Even today, when a historical figure like Joan of Arc is described variously as a saint or
a psychotic, she is known as the "maid" of Orleans and
her virginity is considered an essential element of her
character and, for believers, one reason she was selected
for her heroic mission. Other examples are obvious and
infinite; the point is that there is a long tradition of virginity as an attribute of feminine heroism and an un-
mistakable indication of the elect. With this background
in mind, let us examine the application of the concept
of heroic virginity to romance novels.

The original British Harlequin romances, so wildly
popular that they transformed the publishing industry
in this country and have been translated into dozens of
foreign languages, almost always featured a heroine
who was a virgin. The hero, by contrast, was usually
older and more experienced, and part of the fun, as has
been described elsewhere in this book, was in watching
this inexperienced girl bring her worldly pursuer to
heel. Beyond the concept of the virgin as the pristine

ideal, however, there was an additional and important element in the romances: we as readers anticipated the loss of the heroine's virginity to this one very special man, and in the later books, particularly the American offshoots, we actually saw it.

What is so special about this transition from girlhood to womanhood that it has sold millions of books worldwide and revolutionized the business of bookselling? It's simple: virginity is a gift that can only be given *once,* and it is ideally bestowed on a woman's great love. This giving of virginity adds an immeasurable element of drama and power to a story. It changes the heroine, of course, but in romance novels it also changes the hero.

An example from one of my books *(A Ruling Passion)* which has been the subject of much commentary from both readers and other writers, will serve to illustrate this point. My heroine, a virgin, has just made love for the first time with the hero. She is bleeding slightly, as initiates sometimes do, and when he touches her his fingers come away stained. Then:

> He looked down at them for a moment, and then slowly, ritually, he drew them across his breast from the base of his throat to his shoulder. In a shaft of light from the hall, Megan could see that they left a barely visible trace behind them.
>
> "Now you are truly mine," he whispered.

Obviously, we're getting down to the basics here. Any number of people could go wild with this scene, written eight years ago, from anthropologists talking about defloration ceremonies to biologists talking about animal "marking" and territorial imperatives. But clearly it wouldn't be in the book if the heroine weren't a virgin and if she hadn't just lost that virginity to a man who is very emotionally involved with her. It's the kind of thing I like to do (I'm sure it helps to make my books popular) and it would have to be jettisoned, indeed would never come up, if I were writing about a woman who was already experienced. The power of the narrative, which depends to a large extent on some of these primitive, even cabalistic elements, would be reduced or even removed. It is this very power that animates and distinguishes the story, and the readers love to find it in their books. If I hadn't guessed this from my own youthful imaginings and literary preferences, I would know it from listening to their voices.

More than any Minotaur demanding human sacrifice, they want virgins. Their letters teem with praise for my virginal heroines, even demanding more of them, and when I have sometimes strayed from this ideal for the sake of a little variety I get roundly thumped for it. By contrast, I have never received one letter telling me to "get real" and in tune with today's world by featuring a more experienced protagonist. The readers are in on all of this, they know they're reading fantasy anyway, and they prefer the one in which a virtuous heroine surrenders that virtue, with attendant high drama, to a man who is deeply moved by the gift.

I recall vividly a book signing in which I was approached by a fan who expressed enthusiasm for the loss of virginity theme in my stories, and complained that some of the other series romances were trending toward "women of the world" heroines, a development which she characterized as a "bore." I was amused and delighted when she told me she was a seventy-six-year-old grandmother, had been married three times, and had run away with her first husband at the age of eighteen. Obviously for this woman virginity was a dim memory. She had surrendered hers during the Hoover administration, but she was as enchanted by the mythic appeal of virgins as I was. And when I featured a widow or the survivor of a single love affair as the heroine in some of my later books, she wrote to me and chastised me about it ("Remember me, we met at the Waldenbooks at the Granite Run Mall?"). The enclosed pictures of her several grandchildren were nice, though.

An examination of my royalty statements goes even further to prove this assertion: the books featuring the virginal heroines sell better. Obviously the theme of the virginal heroine who falls deeply in love and then surrenders her virginity to the man she loves is one my readers find as endlessly intriguing as I do. I feel this so strongly that on an occasion early in my writing career when I was desperate to sell anything, I reluctantly left a publishing house because I was being pressured to write differently.

I had sold one series romance to this house, and then was told that what the editor "really wanted" to see next was a book with the theme of the new romance line they were launching, concerning the problems of two married people who separated and then overcame their problems to be reunited at the end of the story. When I replied that I was more comfortable writing the type of romance I had originally sold her, I was told that she already had "enough of those" and needed material for the new line.

Well, I tried. I really did. I cudgeled my brains trying to extract some romantic inspiration from situations like losing a job, being unable to pay the mortgage, dealing with delinquent children, or screaming at a spouse about an extramarital affair (some of the story suggestions offered by this editor, and exactly the sort of thing that readers pick up a romance to escape, in my view). I was then and am now a married person, and I considered that all the above were too close to reality to be the stuff of romance. I certainly would be able to write about such subjects in another context, and in fact have done so quite happily, but not in a book purported to be a series romance! I eventually had to tell the editor that I couldn't do what she wanted. When the proposed line about married people came out, it failed quickly and I felt that my judgment had been vindicated. The readers weren't any more interested than I was.

I may yet get to do my story about the Vestal Virgins (I stopped hearing, "Who wants to read about ancient Rome?" around the time Colleen McCullough's latest offering hit the bestseller list, but the Vestals are still, from an editorial standpoint anyway, something of a stretch). I certainly haven't forgotten it, or its inspiration. The time I spent in that long ago Latin class informed my life, stimulating a fascination with feminine heroism that persists to this day. Sister Charles Eileen, who seemed as old as God to me then but who was probably in her sixties, has, in all likelihood, gone to her eternal reward. For my part, I hope that Boadicea was waiting to greet her.

BRITTANY YOUNG

Making a Choice

Virginity in the Romance

We live in a world where people speak of having sex rather than making love, where sex is invariably linked to violence in movies and in music, where women aren't safe jogging in parks or walking in their own neighborhoods, and where date rape has become commonplace. To women who live and work in this harsh reality, reading the traditional romance offers the opportunity to step for a short time into a fictional world where centuries-old values such as honor, loyalty, integrity, fidelity, and chastity are celebrated. In the traditional romance, there is no confusion or ambiguity surrounding these values. They're an integral part of the story, and the characters live by them.

There are romances of all types—contemporary, historical, series, and non-series—that at times embody these values. But it is in the traditional romance, a short, contemporary romance published primarily by Harlequin and Silhouette in two series, both called simply "Romance," where these values are an essential part of the story and the characters. In these romances there are no explicit love scenes. The writer will, more often than not, take the reader to a certain point in a love scene and then leave the rest to the imagination. And in keeping with old-fashioned values, the lovemaking in the traditional romance usually occurs only within the context of marriage.

These books are romances in the truest and gentlest sense of the word. Sex is neither the center of the plot nor the basis of the relationship between the hero and heroine, though the sexual tension certainly is there with all of its sweet promise. These characters have a deep emotional connection that the reader knows will culminate in marriage; and because of the emotional commitment that evolves over the course of an entire novel, the reader also knows that when the hero and heroine finally *do* make love, their experience will be as exquisite as it should be for people who are truly in love.

The most popular traditional romances share many of the elements that make other types of romance novels popular, such as strong heroes, but there are some elements that are *characteristic* only of the traditional romance. Perhaps the most important—and controversial—of these is the heroine's virginity. Cherished by readers, maligned by critics, it is often misunderstood.

In traditional romances, the heroines are usually virgins when they meet the heroes. That is not to say that the heroine is in any way naive or unsophisticated. Quite the contrary. Her virginity is completely a matter of mature choice—her choice, not that of the men she has dated. She is very clearsighted about her values and doesn't waver because of outside pressure. It takes a particularly strong woman to do that, and it is not until she meets the hero and falls in love with him that she makes the choice to give him the gift of her virginity.

In America today, women are often pressured into having sex when they really don't want to and are confused by changing values and mixed messages. Sex is sometimes treated as casual recreation or as a way to thank one's date for dinner, and as a result it has lost its meaning. Intimacy has been replaced by perfunctoriness. The thrill of the chase, the wonder of first love, has been lost.

In the traditional romance, however, that wonder is recaptured. The hero must pursue the heroine, though often, at the beginning of a book, the hero is interested in the heroine simply for sex. The best authors in this genre can make the chase very exciting. The chase, in fact, is more important than the capture, because the chase is where the romance is.

But it is the heroine who has control over what will and will not happen. Indeed, the heroine in a traditional romance is a study in feminism. She values herself most for qualities that have nothing to do with her sexuality—qualities such as integrity, loyalty, courage, intelligence, generosity of spirit, and, often, a sense of humor. No man will be worthy of her until he recognizes those qualities and until he, himself, values her for them. And the hero must both have strength of character and embody those qualities which make him worthy of her love, traditional qualities that are rapidly becoming easier to find in fiction than in real life.

And that, of course, is the point—to step out of the modern world and its moral confusion into a fictional world where honor and loyalty and chastity are qualities to be celebrated and admired.

BRITTANY YOUNG

Brittany Young is the pseudonym for Sandra Harrison Young. She has published more than twenty-five series romance novels, including the recent release *A Holiday to Remember.* She writes for Silhouette, and her books have been translated into a wide variety of languages and sold abroad.

PENELOPE WILLIAMSON

By Honor Bound

The Heroine as Hero

I truly don't understand why the romance genre is so belittled. Yes, there are romances out there that are silly, under-researched or poorly written, but I'm sure the same could be said for mystery, western and horror books. As a college grad, I wish people would give me more credit for being able to sort out the good writers from the bad. Yet I feel as if I have to put book covers on all the romances I read just to avoid those "why are you reading that trash" comments—as if romances were only one step above comic books.

The woman who penned those words does not write romances; she reads them. It is an excerpt from a letter sent to me by a woman who must have found within my novels a kindred spirit. Whatever the reason, she was moved to write and share her bewilderment that she would be so criticized for her choice of reading material. She thought that I, as a creator of "that trash," would certainly understand and sympathize with her frustration.

And she was right; I do.

I once told my husband that if we come back again as lovers in another life, next time I get to be the man. He didn't laugh. After forty years of this lifetime as a woman, I remain convinced that, although we might have come a long way, this is still a man's world, baby. Romance novels account for roughly 40 percent of all mass market paperback sales, with annual revenues reaching hundreds of millions of dollars. Yet I doubt there is a romance author breathing who hasn't been asked the question: When are you going to write a *real* book? I cannot help but suspect that romance is so often ridiculed and denigrated because it is a literature written almost exclusively by women for women. It is a man's world, after all.

It is a man's world, yes—except in my fantasies.

In the worlds I create in my novels, life is portrayed less as it is and more the way I would like it to be. The fantasies are uniquely *feminine* and the story is essentially the *heroine*'s. She is the one with choices to make, she is the one to take control, to triumph at the end. Yes, she finds love and the man of her dreams (and mine), but the power of choice is ultimately hers. I put her center stage and give her all the heroic qualities usually given to the leading man—she is brave and free spirited, smart and strong willed, honorable and proud. Yet she retains her leading lady role as well, for she is loving and nurturing and sexually alluring. By the end of the book the power is all in my heroine's feminine hands—power over her enemies, over herself, and over the hero, her chosen man.

It is her world, her triumph, her story.

There is an erroneous perception, particularly among men, that romances aren't really novels in the sense of having a story line, but are rather a series of sexual encounters strung together, a sort of lightweight pornography for women. Nothing could be farther from the truth. Pornography is sex without love; in romance, love is center stage. The focus of romance is on the developing relationship between a particular man and woman, who must triumph over seemingly insurmountable obstacles to realize their love for each other. Generally—and many would say realistically—the biggest obstacle faced by the heroine in the story comes from the hero himself.

The heroes in romances are a bit larger than life, but they also possess the very real qualities that women look for in a life-mate. True, he might be drop-dead gorgeous, but I also try to portray him as the type of man who will make a good father and husband. He might be—usually is, in fact—hard-edged and dangerous, but he is also a man of honor and integrity, a man who isn't going to cheat on his wife or run out on her when the going gets rough. But while the hero might be the sort of man who will cook and change diapers and be supportive of his wife's career, he is also a man's man, a dangerous man, who can be tamed by the love of a good woman.

I am intrigued by the fact that most of the heroes, particularly in historical romances, are men with these hard edges. They are often brooding, embittered men with giant chips on their shoulders and hearts encased in steel, men with haunted pasts who have been wounded by life and love. They are hot tempered and proud and stubborn—and very, very vulnerable when it comes to the heroine. She is the one woman, out of all the women in the world, who can teach him how to be happy again, who will introduce him to the wonder and power of love. She brings out his "good" side, his feminine side—his gentleness and compassion and tenderness.

A romance hero is able to be gentle and tender, while at the same time remaining strong and masculine. To me there is something *fierce* about the romance hero. It is the lethal fierceness of a panther stalking his prey, the brave and noble fierceness of an unarmed patriot facing down a tank, the tender fierceness of a father holding his newborn babe in his big hands. The romance hero is exciting and dangerous, and erotic because of it. He pursues the heroine, single-mindedly, relentlessly, just like that panther stalking his prey—and little suspecting that he will be the one caught in the end, that the savage beast will be tamed. A perusal of the bestseller racks proves that readers love these sympathetic, hard-edged men who are conquered by love. We women never meant for sensitive to be equated with wimpy.

The heroine maintains control over her life and destiny by first choosing, and then conquering, her fierce hero. The reader identifies with the heroine and approves of her choice. Along with the heroine, she has fallen in love with the hero—a man who can be both tough and tender, who is strong enough to dominate and control everything in his world except the heroine, the woman he loves almost in spite of himself.

In a romance, the woman has an almost imperceptible upper hand in the relationship. He might be all things to all women, but *she* is the one who gets him. The hero, for all his fierceness, is quite literally brought to his knees to propose marriage and declare his undying love.

The savage beast is tamed by love: such is the allure of the fantasy.

And just what is she like—this woman who is able to have such a devastating and powerful effect on the hero?

She is the kind of woman I would like to have for a daughter, the kind of woman I'd like to imagine that I am, or could be if I were ever tested the way that she is tested. She is a strong, independent woman, perfectly capable of taking care of herself if she must. In the contemporary stories, the heroines usually have careers, they have lives that are full and rich even before the hero emerges on the scene. In historical novels, the heroine is often portrayed as a woman out of step with the repressive society into which she is born. Historical heroines are rebels, hoydens, and they suffer for their spirit and independence—until, that is, the hero comes along to be intrigued by and fall in love with the very qualities that are getting her into so much trouble.

I try to give the heroines in my books the traits and qualities traditionally reserved for the heroes in other types of fiction: honor, loyalty, integrity, courage, intelligence, and good old-fashioned grit. The heroine may begin the book unhappy, even in deadly peril, but she is a survivor. By the story's end her world is in order and her future is rosy because she, along with her hero, have made it that way.

No longer does the hero walk on stage and take control of the story by saving the heroine from the villain's evil clutches. Instead, they meet and surmount danger together. In the process the hero is exposed to the heroine's "heroic" qualities. First he is intrigued, then he offers her a grudging respect, and ultimately he finds himself falling in love with this woman who is so resourceful, so brave, so strong. In romances, the heroine can remain true to herself and still win the love and approbation of a strong man. No matter what trials and tribulations are thrown at the heroine, she emerges at the end of the story strong enough to triumph over it all.

But the hero's own heroic qualities are never threatened or diminished by our heroine's "heroism." He is still allowed the traditional role of protector and provider, while at the same time admitting respect and admiration for the way his woman has proved that she can take care of herself. She is able to have both worlds—she is independent, her own woman, yet at the same time there is a man in her life to stand by her side when the going gets rough. But the fantasy does not stop there. The hero also acknowledges that *she* is there for *him*. By the end of the book there is an ideal union of two equal partners, each respecting the other's abilities, complementing their strengths and weaknesses—a true marriage in the broadest sense of the word.

In a romance, the heroine is able by the end of the book to put, if not her life, then at least her happiness, into the hero's strong and capable hands without surrendering any of her own self-worth and independence. Yes, the hero is physically attracted to the heroine, but he also admires her mind, her spirit, her character. If the writer has done it right, the reader is left with a sense that this hero—whose choice is practically unlimited— has fallen in love with our heroine because of who she is, because of the very *heroic* qualities that caused her to fall in love with him.

As is the case in many fantasies, there is a paradox involved. The heroine is able to be weak and strong, both at the same time. She is able to remain independent while surrendering her heart. But there is no danger to her in this surrendering. Her chosen mate needs her just as much as she needs him.

Once again it is the heroine who is in control; the

choice is hers. Secure in the knowledge that she could, if she had to, take care of herself, she chooses to share her life with a man who is her equal and who recognizes her as such. She has power over him and their world. And nowhere is the heroine's power over her man more evident than in their sexual relationship.

In romance novels, there is no sex for the heroine without her first falling in love. In a sense the entire plot of a romance novel becomes a metaphor for the risk that women take when they fall in love. The heroine meets a man who looks good as a potential lifemate. But there is danger for her: he is fierce, he is stubborn, he could wind up breaking her heart, if not her head. The satisfaction comes when our heroine finally does take the plunge, giving herself wholly, both emotionally and physically, to such a man—and her choice turns out to be the right one. Instead of hurting her, he cherishes her.

In the romantic fantasy the heroine is irresistible to the hero. She does not necessarily have to be beautiful, but she does possess qualities that make her desirable as a life-mate. Practically from the moment he meets her, the hero wants to possess her. Yes, he is attracted by her face and body, but he also becomes intrigued by her spirit. Being an egocentric male, he sees something of himself in her; he sees the hero in her. He begins to imagine her as his perfect complement. While his desire for her might be strictly sexual at first, once the physical bonding takes place, sex is not enough; he must then possess her heart and soul, even while he in turn becomes possessed. The heroine becomes valuable to the man, the one woman out of all the women in the world capable of making him happy, of making his life complete.

In historical romances, where the plot devices of forced or arranged marriages work so well, the heroine's first sexual experience is most often with the hero. But whether the heroine is a sexually ignorant eighteenth-century governess or a twentieth-century widow struggling to raise three children, there remains an aura of purity about her. The heroine rarely if ever has a promiscuous past; she is the "nice girl" our mothers raised us to be. She is a "hero," after all, and heroes traditionally remain pure in thought, word, and deed. She has and always will behave honorably.

Paradoxically, the romantic heroine does not lose her innocence along with her virginity. An aura of purity surrounds her even if there has been another man in her life. Whatever the nature of her past love affair, nobody has ever made love to her quite the way the hero does. Through the hero's lovemaking she discovers the power and potential of her woman's sexuality.

This fantasy parallels and complements the male madonna-whore fantasy found so often in men's fiction. In the male fantasy, the woman can be both a sexual object and the revered wife and mother of his child. She is the demure lady in public who turns into a wild wanton behind the closed bedroom door. But she is only a wanton with her chosen man, and only he can let loose the fiery passions burning within her. In the female version of this fantasy, the woman can enjoy abandoned and passionate sex freely without losing anything of herself, because the act itself is elevated by the depth, power, and above all the *exclusiveness* of the couple's mutual love.

In romances, unlike the heroine, the hero is often sexually experienced. He has known many desirable women; his choice of a marriage partner is virtually unlimited. Yet once he makes love to the heroine, he remains forever bound to her. He can be satisfied by no other woman. Not that he succumbs to this realization easily. He will fight it with all the masculine weapons at his command, a battle that can be waged through 400 pages. But once the hero has met the heroine the outcome is inevitable: he must have her and no other.

This answers a need in woman to believe that the man she loves will desire no others, that he will remain forever faithful and in love with her. This is a fantasy deeply ingrained in the female psyche since the cave days, when the woman relied upon the man to provide food and shelter for her and their children, when his abandonment would mean almost certain death. If she could keep her man tied to her with her sexual allure, she would be assured of a provider and protector in the personal sense, and in the larger sense the species would be propagated.

In a romance novel the heroine is able to keep the man committed and faithful through sex, yet at the same time retain her aura of innocence and purity, and her heroic integrity, which was what made her valuable and desirable to him in the first place. Once again, the power is in the woman's hands—*she* does the choosing of her mate and *she* maintains control over him through her heroism and her irresistible sexuality, which remains forever unsullied and therefore of value no matter how many times she participates in the sex act. But the fantasy does not stop there, for the sex act leads to a rebirth for the hero. A man meets a woman, a strong, courageous, honorable woman, a *heroic* woman, and through the act of loving her, he is uplifted, enhanced, made complete.

To me this is the ultimate romantic fantasy: that the

hero is changed, made somehow more *heroic,* through being loved by a heroic woman. For all his strength and independence, for all his hard edges, there almost always comes a point in today's romance novel when the hero acknowledges to the heroine that his life would cease to have meaning if she were to leave him. The hero has been given a new life, and it is the heroine who has given it to him.

This is a heady fantasy for women who have been conditioned for centuries to wait for the man to come to her, to believe that only a man can give meaning to her life, that only a man can give a woman worth. How extraordinary to think that women can be heroes. And that men need women just as much, if not more, than we need them.

PENELOPE WILLIAMSON

Penelope Williamson has published five historical romance novels. Her fourth, *A Wild Yearning,* was honored as Best Historical Romance in a series by Romance Writers of America. Her fifth, *Keeper of the Dream,* was published as a lead title by Dell in 1992. She has written for both Dell and Avon.

Ms. Williamson holds a bachelor's degree in history from the University of Idaho and a master's degree in journalism from American University. She worked in the fields of journalism and public relations for fifteen years before beginning her writing career.

JUDITH ARNOLD

Women Do

In my mind I picture a billboard, an advertisement for a film. The artwork recedes but the words remain clear: "A daring spy. A demonic plot to end the world. A beautiful girl." Or perhaps it says: "Crime stalks the city. He's a brave cop. She's in danger."

Maybe it's not a movie billboard. Maybe it's an advertisement for a book: "A western lawman. A ruthless oil baron. The woman they both want." Or maybe it's a critique of a short-story collection in a spring 1991 edition of the *New York Times Book Review,* in which a story's hero is described as a war veteran currently operating a ranch and the heroine is described as his neighbor and sometime lover.

I call it the "Man *does,* Woman *is*" syndrome: the male character is defined by what he does, the female character by what she is. This syndrome seems to afflict a large proportion of our popular entertainment. In movies, television shows, and commercial fiction, far too often the hero is the active character, charging through life and making things happen while the heroine reacts, or is acted upon, or in some way motivates the hero's actions.

All good fiction is, to some extent, about

character. Romance fiction places a particular emphasis on character—specifically, on a hero and heroine who meet, struggle with their feelings for each other, and ultimately triumph over their differences, establishing a common ground on which to build a life together. But the standard plot of a romance novel cannot be summed up with the cliché "Boy meets girl, boy loses girl, boy gets girl." In the romance fiction I write, the *girl* does the meeting, losing, and getting. The woman *does*.

I first started reading romance novels in 1982. At the time, I was looking for a way to earn money as a novelist, and I figured my best bet would be to investigate commercial genre fiction. I did not expect to like the four romance novels I selected at random off a rack. I assumed they would promote the notion that a woman was dependent on a man to give her life meaning and joy—that without a man, a woman was incomplete. My intention was to buy a few of these novels, read them, and then move on to other genres of commercial fiction which I believed would be more compatible with my feminist views.

I bought four contemporary romances, read them—and didn't move on.

I can't say I adored all four books, nor can I say I've adored every romance novel I've read since then. The variety among romance novels is enormous. Yet those first four books excited me, inspired me, made me want to sit down and write a romance novel of my own.

Why? Because in those books, the heroines *did*.

The heroines I create take steps, hold opinions, and move forward into the world, blazing their own paths through life. They cannot simply be described as "a beautiful girl" or "a woman in danger" or "a neighbor and sometime lover." What the heroine does, not what she is, lies at the heart of the novels I write.

What do my heroines do?

They work. They may be carefully mapping out a career or simply holding down a job. Either way, they make ends meet. If they haven't got a paying job, they still labor at something—raising children, pursuing volunteer activities, seeking solutions. They are rarely idle.

The heroines of my novels sense a need for something and go after it. The "something" they need isn't necessarily love; in fact, love is usually the last thing they're looking for. They may be searching for a tangible object, financial security, a home for their family, even something as nebulous as contentment. Whatever they're after, they recognize their lack and strive to overcome it. They don't stand around hoping for someone to come along and provide them with the missing pieces.

The heroines who populate my books believe. They harbor vast quantities of faith—in themselves, in the future, in humanity, in the power to do good in the world. No matter how difficult their lives have been or how many scars they bear, they don't give up hope. They may be in retreat as a novel opens, but by the end they have recovered their faith and set their sights accordingly. It is surely an act of faith to open oneself to intimacy. I create heroines strong enough to take that perilous step, to trust themselves and those around them, to make themselves vulnerable to love.

My heroines never wallow in self-pity. If a heroine has had a bad love affair in the past, she is done with it before the novel begins. The tedious tribulations of the breakup are history by the time the reader meets her. Many feminist novels of the 1960s and 1970s dealt with heroines struggling to extricate themselves from unsatisfying relationships. For those feminist heroines, freeing oneself from a dreary or abusive love affair was an end in itself, a symbol of liberation and growth. In my books the heroines are already liberated and growing by the time the reader meets them. Their past experiences may have left a few emotional bruises, but the reader doesn't have to bear witness while the heroines wring their hands helplessly.

In fact, even if my heroines wanted to wring their hands, they wouldn't have the time. They are too busy—feeding their kids, taking care of their siblings, completing their education, earning a living, repairing the back porch—*doing*. Their lives are ordered on pragmatism and common sense. They direct their energies outward—into work, into play, and into relationships.

Recent studies from Wellesley College's Stone Center for Developmental Studies and Services have explored the theory that female psychology doesn't necessarily follow the male model of human development, which holds that maturity is reached through separation and autonomy. Instead, Stone Center studies have found that healthy women reach maturity not by severing relationships but by forging them.

Many men—including those who disdain romance fiction—would no doubt claim that the female model is inferior to the male model. Eager to be viewed by men as equals, some feminists might agree. Those of use who admire romance fiction would argue that the ability to establish and nurture relationships is as valid and as valuable as the ability to scale mountains alone. It is also a good deal more practical, since we live in a crowded world in which cooperation is the only viable route to survival. If we can't learn to love one another, we doom our species.

This, to me, is the most important thing my heroines do: they connect with others.

Given the nature of romance, the primary connection my heroines make is to heroes. But my books convey an underlying message: men and women are in many ways as alien to each other as the East and the West of the Cold War era, as the Jews and Palestinians of the Middle East, as the Catholics and Protestants of Belfast, and the members of different ethnic and racial groups in our own country. Yet if, despite their differences, a man and a woman can somehow build a bridge across the chasm that separates them and create a real and vital connection, then the world can be saved. If a man and a woman can learn to compromise, negotiate, and understand each other, anything is possible.

The unions formed between the heroines and heroes in my books reflect in microcosm the truth that people must learn to live with and love one another for the sake of the earth's future. Back in the 1960s, when the Beatles told us all we needed was love, they were singing not only about romantic love but about world peace. The romance novels I write offer a symbolic illustration of that concept, showing a hero and heroine at odds with each other, misunderstanding each other, working at cross purposes—but ultimately discovering that moving toward mutual respect and affinity will bring them much greater happiness than distrust and strife ever can.

Of course, a romance novel is not just about a heroine *doing*. She has to interact with the hero. Is it necessary to counterbalance heroines who *do* by pairing them with heroes who simply *are*? Does the existence of a strong, dominant heroine preclude the existence of a strong, dominant hero?

Quite the contrary. I am bemused by the many movies, television shows, male-oriented genre fiction, and other popular entertainments that feature an allegedly strong hero paired with a passive heroine whose role is so negligible she is aptly referred to as the "love interest." I call these heroes *allegedly* strong because I believe that any hero who would choose as his partner so ineffectual and shallow a woman betrays a weakness in himself. Real men aren't afraid of strong women.

In the novels I write, the hero is as active as the heroine. He can keep up with her. He can't surpass her, though—and he possesses enough self-confidence not to let that fact bother him.

Reflecting the wide variety in taste among readers, romance heroes vary greatly, ranging from inscrutably macho to unabashedly sensitive. The heroes I've created run the gamut: at one end of the spectrum, in *One Good Turn* (published by Harlequin) the hero falls in love with a rape victim who has channeled her anger into a successful career as a prosecuting attorney. The hero must renew her faith in heterosexual love. At the other end of the spectrum, in *Survivors* (also published by Harlequin) the hero is a brutalized Vietnam War veteran, given to violent flashbacks, who needs the heroine to renew *his* faith in the goodness of humankind. Between those two extremes lie fathers and sons, gentlemen and rogues, professionals and laborers, cops and even a felon.

Like the vast majority of heroes in popular fiction, film, and television, the heroes of my books are strong and dynamic. What makes a hero particularly suited to one of my novels, however, is his uncompromising love for the heroine.

He may resist that love; he may try to wish it away. He may behave in a manner that hurts the heroine, but he does so out of love for her.

He is comfortable in his masculinity. Passive women bore him. Active women excite him; he doesn't feel threatened by a woman's strength.

He also happens to be wonderful in bed. No need to be coy: the eroticism of romance novels is one of their most enjoyable aspects. In the novels I write, it is a given that a woman is entitled to sexual satisfaction and that a real man can't be fulfilled unless his partner is also fulfilled. Not every amorous encounter culminates in ecstasy all around—but the key is that if the heroine isn't satisfied, neither is the hero.

The heroes I create want to gratify their women—and unlike so many mainstream novels, where the man's prowess is assumed but never explained or proven, the erotic scenes in most contemporary romances are written in lush detail, offering ample evidence that the heroes are putting forth a genuine effort to succeed as lovers. Sex is depicted as a healthy, rapturous communion between two adults. No one partner is supposed to get more out of it than the other. When the experience isn't shared equally, it is considered a failure, a conflict that requires resolution.

Unrealistic? Maybe—but I would contend that the problem lies not with romance novels but with reality. Rather than deride the idealized sexuality of romance novels, critics might be better off questioning why lovers in real life don't exert themselves more to attain that ideal of mutual satisfaction.

The novels I write arise from a solidly feminist perspective. They center on heroines who have structured useful, challenging lives for themselves and on heroes who welcome these heroines as their equals. They allow for human frailties and genuine misunderstandings; they offer imperfect but likable characters who aspire to improve themselves and who are generous enough to forgive the flaws in those they love. The hero needs the heroine as much as she needs him, and the bond they ultimately form is a balanced one.

Why are romance novels ridiculed? Why do feminists shy from them? Why do men laugh at them?

The novels I write don't revolve around material achievement, domination, or conquest—the standards by which we tend to gauge success in our male-dominated society. My books aren't about proving one-self in battle, or measuring one's legitimacy by how high one has climbed on the corporate ladder, or calibrating success according to how many rivals one has defeated.

I can't help but think that the Stone Center researchers got it right when they postulated that women mature differently from men. Women assess their worth by other criteria: how much they contribute to the well-being of others; how successfully they navigate the complex world of relationships; how solid a grounding they provide for the generations that will inherit the planet—and how wholesome a planet those generations will inherit.

To belittle romance fiction is to belittle women. To read romance fiction is to confront the strength of women, the variety of their experience, and the validity of their aspirations and accomplishments. To appreciate the kind of romance fiction I write is to admit that women can *do,* and that given the opportunity, they can change the world for the better.

JUDITH ARNOLD (ARIEL BERK)

Judith Arnold is a pseudonym for Barbara Keiler. She also writes as Ariel Berk. She is the author of over forty series romance novels, with more than four million copies of her books in print. Her publishers include Harlequin, Silhouette, and Berkley/Jove. Several of her books, including *A Package Deal,* have appeared on the Waldenbooks Romance bestseller list. Among her numerous awards is the Critics Choice Award from *Romantic Times* magazine for *Comfort and Joy.* Another of her titles, *Remedies of the Heart,* was a finalist for the Romance Writers of America Golden Medallion award.

Ms. Keiler is a graduate of Smith College and holds a master's degree in creative writing from Brown University. She originally pursued a career as a playwright, and her plays have been staged professionally in New York City, Washington, DC, San Francisco, and elsewhere. She has received writing fellowships from the Shubert Foundation and the National Endowment for the Arts. She has taught at a number of colleges and universities around the country including Brown University, California State University at Chico, and the State University of New York system.

STELLA CAMERON

Moments of Power

The temptation in embarking on this discussion is to fire statistics—and there are many of them—that back up what is already well known: romance novels command a whopping share of the fiction market. But my task here is to put forth not the what, but the why in the issue. Why do so many women read so many romance novels? Why have so many women read so many romance novels for so long? And why do they continue to do so despite widespread and insulting ridicule?

We have only to consider the obstacles women have overcome in, say, the last hundred years to find a yardstick of their stamina in the face of adversity. An oppressed group who, through unwavering determination and a staggering degree of courage—and at great personal cost—have propelled themselves from classified chattel into high office and respected fields throughout much of the world is unlikely to tolerate being told what they should and should not read. The fiction that such women choose to read in the face of relentless disapproval clearly must have a strong appeal.

A major portion of that appeal is readily experienced by the romance reader in the two climactic moments that occur in every good romance novel. Neither of these fictional climaxes has anything to do with sex; both have everything to do with power. The first climactic point occurs when the hero acknowledges the heroine's heroic qualities. At that moment he begins his fall into love, a surrender that gives the heroine power over him. The second climactic moment occurs when the heroine uses her power over the hero to teach him how to love.

To understand these moments of power in the novels one has to understand a very special aspect of romance fiction. These are books that present women's view of women. Historically in fiction women have seen themselves watched by men, reported by men, second-guessed by men. But in the romance novel women celebrate the heroic qualities they think are most important in their own sex: honor, courage, intelligence, integrity. In a romance novel the heroine may be beautiful, but her beauty is a side issue, not an important aspect of her nature. The hero may be attracted to her initially because of her beauty, but the heroine will not accept him until he has recognized her heroic qualities. These are the true qualities that define her, the qualities she considers important. Part of the definition of a hero is that he is a man who is capable of recognizing and appreciating these qualities.

The scene in which the hero recognizes the heroine's heroic traits—traits that heretofore he has believed were exclusive to the male of the species—is always a memorable one in a romance novel. In my first historical romance for Avon Books the hero, Edward, Viscount Hawkesly, is forced to deal with the true nature of Lindsay Granville, the woman he initially believed he could use as a tool to gain vengeance. After achieving his goal he had planned to relegate the heroine to his country estates where she would languish out of sight and out of mind. But all that changes when her courage and sense of honor are revealed. This climactic moment occurs when he discovers that she has been risking her neck engaging in highly dangerous activities designed to preserve the inheritance of her dead brother's infant son. Hawkesly can no longer dismiss Lindsay as an amusing nonentity or a pretty little plaything to be used and discarded. She is a *heroine*. His awe of her increases even more when he realizes that, in spite of his misjudgment and misuse of her, Lindsay's capacity for loving him is great enough to allow her to grant forgiveness. It is the hero's recognition and admiration of the heroine's noble qualities that inspire his love for her and give her power over him.

The second turning point of the novels occurs when the heroine uses her power to change the hero. In order to understand that climactic moment, one must know something about romance novel heroes.

The romance hero is often portrayed as a dark force, vaguely satanic, perhaps. He may be aloof, introspective, and sardonic. He may be recovering from a previous relationship with a woman who was not "worthy" and who, therefore, could not be with and for him what the heroine could be. He may be accustomed to exercising a rigid control over his emotions. He may have a capacity for plotting ruthless vengeance.

All of this male's dangerously exciting darkness is seen as the result of never having truly been loved or of having had his own love thwarted. In effect he has lost his ability to love. All he needs to bring out a will to love that is stronger than his will to be tough and independent is the love of the only woman meant for him. This is our heroine, the one woman who has the power to give him back or help him rediscover his ability to love. Although initially he may see love as a weakness and resist succumbing to it, by the end of the book the hero realizes that without love his life is incomplete. He understands that the heroine's love and, equally important, her restoration of his ability to love have made him whole. The heroine has tamed the dark side of his nature, uncovered his innate nobility, revealed his underlying integrity. In short, she allows him to be all that he can be.

Thus the novel reaches its second intoxicating climax, the point at which the heroine uses the power she has over the hero to restore to him his ability to love. In essence she influences him to use his own heroic powers in a positive rather than a destructive manner. In Amanda Quick's *Scandal*, the hero abandons his goal of pitiless vengeance against the heroine's family when he surrenders to love. He finds himself actually rescuing her scapegrace brothers and dealing with her feckless father instead of ruining him. Ultimately he uses his power to help solve the family's problems rather than destroy the whole clan as he had originally intended. And he does so because of the heroine's influence.

The worthy heroine thus becomes the strongest force for good in the life of the strong man she chooses to love. There is no sweeter victory, and every romance reader revels in it.

Romances have existed and continue to exist because they are a joyous celebration of the strengths women value most within themselves. Romance novels underscore what many women believe: love and by extension sex are not death but birth, not loss but gain. In romance novels love is portrayed as an adventure embarked upon by free, bold women who know that their true power lies in their own heroic qualities.

STELLA CAMERON

Stella Cameron is the author of more than twenty-five series romance and romantic-suspense novels published by Harlequin. Her first historical romance, *Only by Your Touch*, was published in 1992 by Avon. Her books have been honored by the Pacific Northwest Writers' Conference and Romance Writers of America. Among her titles which have appeared on the Waldenbooks Romance bestseller list is *No Stranger*. She combines teaching and speaking engagements with her writing career and has held such positions as Writer-in-Residence for the University of Montana at Western Montana College.

SANDRA BROWN

The Risk of Seduction and the Seduction of Risk

For weeks I deliberated over how to approach this essay. I wished to write something highly intellectual, something enlightening, a treatise which would reveal the stunning secret behind the enduring success of the romance genre. But even to myself, after I mentally signaled for the drum roll, whisked away the satin cloth and said, "Ta-da!" what did I reveal?

Romances are fun.

There. In five syllables I've covered my topic. The reason romances have endured, essentially from the time humankind began grunting out stories about heroes and heroines, is because *they are fun*—fun to write, fun to read, fun to dissect and discuss. Nothing further should be required to explain the popularity of the genre. Bubble gum is fun. Fireworks are fun. Roller coasters and ferris wheels are fun. They serve no real purpose. Neither do they fill a void in the grand scheme of things. To my knowledge, no one has ever analyzed why they're *there*. They exist solely to entertain.

The entertainment factor itself is reason enough for the romance genre to have emerged, survived, and evolved into its present form. But since I was asked to contribute an essay longer than the last 280 words, I was expected to explore *why* romances are fun. What has made them appealing for generations? In a contemporary world peopled by skeptics and cynics, why does their popularity continue?

Well, even skeptics and cynics fantasize, don't they? That, in this writer's opinion, is the foundation of the genre's allure. Romances present basic fantasies, fantasies that appeal to large numbers of women. Successful writers are able to recreate those fantasies with the most powerful appeal to the imagination of their readers. Is there any harm in that? I don't think so.

Even as a very young child, I didn't really believe in Santa Claus. I desperately wanted to. I went along when my mother and daddy put out carrots for the reindeer and cookies and milk for Santa. When they stared heavenward and pointed at imaginary twinkling lights streaking across the sky, I swore I saw them, too. I pretended to hear sleigh bells on the roof. But deep down, I was thinking, "Come on, guys. A fat man in a furry red suit makes it to every house all over the world in one night?! Give me a break." Intuitively, I knew it was make believe. It was play-like. It was all in fun.

Bingo, we're back to the appeal of romances. It's enjoyable to believe, even temporarily, that fabulous things can happen. The reader wants to be drawn into a fantasy where all the trials and tribulations of life will be resolved.

Fantasies grant us momentary permission to be something that we're not. A Louis L'Amour western allows its reader to be a tough but compassionate cowboy for a day. During the hours readers are engrossed in the story, they adopt the honor code of the Old West. They have keen eyes and quick hands and the fearful respect of their adversaries. This hardly means that any reader is going to put the book aside, buy a horse and a Colt .45, and strike out for the badlands. It's make believe. It's fun. The western novels of Louis L'Amour transport readers to another time and place. While visiting there, they possess the same praiseworthy traits of L'Amour's heroes, and perhaps some seedy characteristics of the bad guys, too.

Likewise, romances allow their readers to "try on" different characteristics. A shy reader might enjoy reading about a heroine who is self-assertive and confident. A reader with a melancholy disposition might like reading about a heroine with a biting sense of humor. As for myself, I'm a coward. Perhaps that's why I often force my heroines to exhibit tremendous courage in the face of disaster. They meet head-on situations that I would avoid at all costs. They challenge foes that would have me cowed and begging for mercy. In *Slow Heat in Heaven* I vicariously confronted one of my worst fears—a snake.

In our fantasy life we can climb into somebody else's skin for a while, move around in it and see how it feels, play mental "dress-up." Among my colleagues, it's generally known that I come from a conservative background. I was reared to believe in traditional values and to adhere strictly to Judeo-Christian morals. Recently one of my colleagues asked me, "In light of your upbringing, how do you account for your villains and villainesses? They're so slimy you could skim oil off them." Taking that as a compliment, I laughed and replied that I was finally getting a change to be a bad girl, or a bad boy. Being the oldest of five children, I was expected to set an example for my younger siblings. Now, through my work, my dark, unexplored nature frequently rears its ugly head. It's great fun, letting the Devil have his way with my characters. This does not mean that *I* plan to shed my moral convictions, run amok, and commit mayhem or murder.

Nor will my reader after she reads one of my novels. The books are a departure into another world. The characters are figments of my imagination. Moving for a time in their world is like putting on a Halloween costume. I'm not going to assume that persona forever, but it's fun to pretend for a while that I'm someone totally different from who I really am.

Haven't we all entertained the notion of being Scarlett O'Hara? Who reads an Ian Fleming book without mentally walking in 007's shoes? If escaping the fantasy becomes a problem, it arises from the psyche of the reader and not from the romances. Hershey can hardly be blamed for a chocolate eater's obesity. In the course of my twelve-year writing experience, I have not heard of a single instance where a reader became dissatisfied with her life because she read romance fiction. In fact, my fan mail supports the opposite. Readers write to say something like, "I shared pages 125 through 130 with my husband last night. He liked them, too. *Thanks!*"

By now I hope I've made a convincing argument that romances are fun because they appeal to the readers' fantasy life, which, granted, is more active in some individuals than in others.

One of my award-winning books, *Honor Bound,* demonstrates how fantasies are incorporated into and actually assist in developing plots. In the first chapter the hero, an American Indian activist, escapes from prison and takes the heroine hostage. This pseudo-bondage theme is next-door neighbor to those made popular in Victorian erotica, with one vital distinction—

there is no pain, blood, or humiliation. In a romance, the kidnapper is noble, doing the wrong thing but for the right reason. The elements of danger and helplessness are more suggestion than fact, and, at the end of *Honor Bound,* the hero actually rescues the heroine from dismal unhappiness. Because this particular hero is an American Indian who comes from a disadvantaged background (he was raised on a reservation) and the heroine is a WASP whose family has wealth and social position, *Honor Bound* incorporates a form of the Cinderella fantasy, in which characters from very different worlds can conquer deeply ingrained prejudices and fall in love.

Shortly after the kidnapping (and a tempestuous seduction), the hero is recaptured and sent back to prison to complete the remaining year of his sentence. Following his release, he returns to the heroine to apologize for the ordeal he had put her through. He is shocked to learn that, in the interim, she has borne him a son. This fantasy, in which a man returns to a woman he cannot forget only to discover that she has borne him a child, is very popular with romance readers. In romance, the child manifests the emotional bond that has been forged between the hero and heroine. The reader gets additional pleasure from watching the tough-guy hero crumble at the sight, smell, and sound of a baby. Didn't we all get mushy when Tom Selleck, Steve Guttenburg, and Ted Danson came to love the child abandoned on their doorstep in the movie *Three Men and a Baby?*

In *Honor Bound* the hero's father was an Anglo soldier who abandoned his reservation-bred mother after his conception. Embittered by that, the hero refuses to allow his son to grow up without a father and demands that the heroine marry him. The marriage of convenience is one of the most popular romance fantasies. In a marriage of convenience, the hero and heroine are legally married and they live together, but they are relative strangers. They must still go through their courtship, a courtship given a special piquancy because it is conducted within marriage.

Mind you, as I was writing this story I didn't consciously incorporate these fantasies for the benefit of my reader. Subconsciously, I was pleasing myself. In reality, being kidnapped and seduced would be terrifying and traumatizing, an experience from which one would never recover. *But this was make believe!* The kidnapper was the dashing and daring Lucas Greywolf, imprisoned for a crime he didn't commit. He was dangerous and volatile, but he was also a tortured soul to whom Aislinn taught tenderness and trust. She taught him how to love. And on that mountaintop, when Lucas, angry and anguished, his silver earring glimmering in the moonlight, seduced Aislinn, I was *there.*

And therein is the crux of what makes fantasies fun. In fantasy, no matter how exciting, how dangerous our experiences are, we are always safe. We can be both the seducer and the seduced without having to account for our actions within the fantasy. Involved but detached, we can watch the characters struggle to release themselves from the consequences of their misguided deeds without having to suffer those consequences ourselves. We can have all the fun without ever having to pay the penalties.

Why has the immense popularity of romances endured? They're fiction. They're fantasy. They're *fun.*

SANDRA BROWN

Sandra Brown has published over fifty novels and currently has over 12 million copies of her books in print worldwide. Her list of books includes both series romances, one of which, *22 Indigo Place,* appeared on the *New York Times* bestseller list, and ten single title releases.

Ms. Brown has received numerous awards from romance trade magazines and from organizations of fans and writers as well as sales awards from the Waldenbooks and B. Dalton bookstores. Her titles consistently appear on major bestseller lists, including the *New York Times, Washington Post, Los Angeles Times,* and *Publishers Weekly* lists. Her novels also appear regularly on the Waldenbooks and B. Dalton bestseller lists.

In August 1991 three of Ms. Brown's novels, *Texas! Sage, Breath of Scandal,* and *Texas! Chase,* appeared on the *New York Times* list at the same time, a distinction shared with only three other writers. Ms. Brown's former occupations include modeling and work in commercial television.

SUZANNE SIMMONS GUNTRUM

Happily Ever After

The Ending as Beginning

I never wanted to be a romance writer.

In fact, at nine I wanted to be Loretta Young. At eleven I saw myself as a Risë Stevens or a Van Cliburn. At fourteen I was determined to become the new, young, female Dag Hammarskjöld (who happened to be secretary general of the United Nations back in those days). At seventeen I wanted desperately to go on the stage (Broadway, here I come!).

In college I first decided law was for me, perhaps one day the Supreme Court. Then I switched my major to English Literature. I would teach Chaucer and Milton, I told myself—brilliantly, of course, and with new insight. I would live on the sacred grounds of some university and spend my life ensconced in academia, as my father had.

I celebrated my twenty-first birthday, graduated from college, and married—all in the same week. In the years that followed I worked as a high school English teacher, an employment counselor, and a business supervisor for Bell Telephone. Then I had a baby and decided it was time to write serious fiction.

Initially I tried meaning-filled short stories. (They were, at best, terribly earnest.)

I tried poetry next. To date I've written one poem.

Then, while I was living in a small Indiana town, a neighbor handed me a Harlequin romance by the inimitable Roberta Leigh and said those famous words: "Maybe you can write one of these." I was horrified by the suggestion. This was 1975. I wouldn't be caught dead *reading* a silly romance novel, much less *writing* one. I've lived to eat my own words. Every last one.

From the first, I was hooked. In the ensuing years I have read hundreds of romance novels. I've written more than twenty-five. And when I sat down to write this piece I asked myself several questions: What is the appeal of the hero and heroine in a romance novel? How do we recognize them right from the start? (Because we always do.) And why do we, the readers, enjoy these books so much?

What tips off the reader right from the start about the hero and the heroine? Language for one thing. Attitude and actions, for another.

I looked at my own historical romance, *Desert Rogue*, and realized that the hero is the *tallest* man in the book, he has the *broadest* shoulders, the *bluest* eyes, and the *darkest* hair. The hero is also the man who lives on the edge. He is fundamentally uncivilized and untamed. He is primal. He is primitive. He is man as warrior.

British aristocrat? Sometimes. Halfbreed? Sometimes. Outcast? Sometimes. Wild man? Sometimes. Gunfighter? Gambler? Sometimes. Tinker, tailor, soldier, spy? Sometimes.

Honorable? Always. A man of his word? Always. A man who dares? Always. A man of action? Always. A man desperately in need of love? Always, even if he doesn't admit it to himself.

And the only one who recognizes that he is in need of love is the heroine. She sees him as a man to be tamed through her love—not into a lapdog but into a strong, responsive male who will be her partner for the rest of their lives and for whatever comes after. She believes in him when no one else would, or does, or dares. The heroine is the woman who dares. The heroine is also an intelligent woman, an honorable woman, a brave woman. (Don't forget, she is the only one who *dares* to love the hero.) Frankly, it takes a lot of guts to be the heroine of a romance novel.

Why do we, the readers, enjoy these books so much? Obviously we enjoy reading about challenging men and gutsy heroines. We also read romance novels because they're fun. Because they give us immense pleasure and joy. Because in the end there is no ambiguity, no tragedy, no defeat. There is ambiguity enough, tragedy enough, defeat enough in real life. We do not read romances to be reminded of these realities.

In a romance novel we know that, whatever the odds against them, the hero and heroine will come together in the end and live happily ever after. Indeed, if the above is *not* true, then either the book is flawed or it isn't a romance.

So why read a novel when we already know how it is going to end? Because it is the process, not the conclusion, that we are reading for. Indeed, it is *safe* for us to enjoy the process because we are already guaranteed of the ending. (The same can be said for the mystery novel. We know the crime/puzzle will be solved by the last page. Therefore, we can sit back and enjoy the ride.)

What is so satisfying about the process in a romance

novel? I've thought long and hard about this question and I think I have the answer. The romance novel provides its reader with a safe way to experience the broad range of emotions, both male and female, both the hero's and the heroine's, associated with the roller coaster ride of falling in love.

I looked at my own published books and realized that my World War I love story, *The Golden Raintree,* has had the greatest emotional impact on my readers, has generated the most fan mail, has drawn the most impassioned response from complete strangers at conferences and autographings.

Why?

Because the potential for tragedy and defeat is so great in the love story of James and Christine. He is an American soldier who goes off to fight in the trenches of Europe. She is a devout Quaker who is morally opposed to violence and war. The backdrop of their romance is bittersweet, intense, even horrific at times.

War *is* a matter of life and death. War *is* horrific. The only thing that makes it bearable in a romance novel is the certain knowledge that there will be a happy ending. Therefore, the reader knows, before she even opens to the first page, that she can let herself experience the gamut of emotions.

Let me tell you a true story. I gave a copy of *The Golden Raintree* to my neighbor. She isn't a romance reader. She didn't know that a happy ending is guaranteed. Halfway through the book she called me up and blurted out: "Sue, I can't read another word until I know that James isn't going to be killed in the war, until you promise me that everything is going to be okay in the end."

I promised.

It is a promise every romance reader expects when she picks up a romance novel: The hero and the heroine will be together in the end. They will live happily ever after.

SUZANNE SIMMONS GUNTRAM (SUZANNE SIMMONS, SUZANNE SIMMS)

Suzanne Guntrum has had over twenty-five series romances published by Dell, Silhouette, and Harlequin. Her first historical romance, *Desert Rogue,* will be published by Avon under her pseudonym, Suzanne Simmons. Several of her books have appeared on the Waldenbooks Romance bestseller list including *As Night Follows Day* and *A Wild Sweet Magic.* One of her titles, *Of Passion Born,* was honored by *Romantic Times* magazine as the Silhouette Desire of the Year.

Ms. Guntrum has a degree in Medieval English Literature from Pennsylvania State University. Before pursuing a full-time writing career, she taught high school English and then went to work in management at AT&T. She combines speaking engagements with her writing and has lectured at the Midwest Writers Workshop at Ball State University.

DIANA PALMER

Let Me Tell You About My Readers

It is ironic that romance appeals to almost everyone, but in literature it is something of a ragged stepchild and needs defending. I find it fascinating that the other genres—mystery, horror, science fiction, fantasy, suspense, and western—never have to be justified or explained. Yet romance novels, the revenues from which comprise the bedrock earnings of a large segment of the publishing industry, seem always to stand in need of defense. Critics of the books are legion.

But it is not the critics who matter to me. It is my readers. The women for whom I produce my books are women just like me. Let me tell you about them.

Although I have readers from every walk of life and many of them are much better educated than I ever expect to be, the majority of my readership represents the hard-working labor force. They are women who spend eight grueling hours a day in a garment factory, in front of a classroom, or behind a desk. Most of them are married and have children. Some are divorced or widowed. These hard-working women leave their jobs at the end of the day and pick up their children at day-care centers. They go home to a house that needs cleaning, to dishes that need washing, to meals that have to be prepared. They go home to dirty clothes that must be washed, to organizational tasks that include making sure the kids are bathed and the homework is done.

These women all have one basic thing in common: they know what love is. They live it every day. They sacrifice for their families, they worry, they fuss, but most of them would do it all over again. Family life is as basic a need in some women as life itself.

Romance novels allow these women, who have experienced love and its aftermath, to be many things. They allow them to be virgins again. To be career women. To be debutantes. To be princesses. To live in luxury and even, sometimes, in decadence. The novels allow them to escape the normal cares and woes of life by returning in dreams to a time less filled with responsibilities. Romances allow them to experience all this and more without risking what they already have.

Is fantasy healthy? Does it, as some claim, provide a dangerous escape from problems that are better faced? Some small percentage of any society is susceptible to obsession. Just as some people are addicted to alcohol and drugs, others become addicted to fantasy and withdraw into it to the detriment of their own lives. But for the majority, daydreams can be a very healthy occupation because they enable people to step back from problems that threaten to be overwhelming. They provide breathing room and the opportunity to see obstacles from a safe distance.

My reader mail includes letters from people who have been suicidal, who have suffered serious health problems, who have nursed children with fatal or debilitating defects. These readers tell me that my books and those of other romance authors have helped them get through periods of anguish and grief. In fact, romance novels have many times kept *me* going during the trials and tribulations of my own life. The books do this by providing a brief respite that allows readers to gather their energies so that they can return, refreshed, to face and solve real-life problems. Total escape cannot be healthy. But a breathing space can save one's sanity. Romantic fantasy is a safety valve, a way of letting off steam without boiling any water.

As long as men and women fall in love, romance will continue to thrive. In spite of criticism and ridicule, mockery and disdain, artificial insemination notwithstanding and critics taken into consideration, young girls will secretly dream of young men coming to woo them even if those young girls grow up to become theoretical physicists. Married women will dream of a rich suitor coming to carry them off in a Rolls, a bouquet of roses in one hand, a bottle of champagne in the other, and a promise of deathless passion on his lips. Old women will dream of green meadows and long kisses in the sunshine long after arthritic joints make such pastimes uncomfortable. Cinderella, Beauty and the Beast, and Sleeping Beauty are as eternal as life itself, impervious to reality. Love triumphant with a happy ending. There are so few untarnished things in the real world.

I make no apologies for my choice of vocation. I make no excuses for the type of fiction I choose to write. I produce fantasy for people who need a one-hour escape from reality. I work for the mother of a child with cystic fibrosis who has had to sit up all night alone looking after him. For the wife of a dying paraplegic whose vigil is almost at an end. For the factory worker whose feet hurt. For the teacher who comes home at the end of a trying day to face unswept floors, uncooked meals, and the endless paperwork required of her profession. For the sick woman in the nursing home whose family come to see her once a month. For the farm wife with five children who cheerfully goes about her chores to earn herself a quiet hour in bed when everyone else is asleep. And during that hour she can wear a ball gown instead of an apron, glass slippers instead of faded bedroom shoes.

For all those women, I write books. They are my family, my fans, my friends. I know many of them by name. They write to me and I write back. I remember them in my prayers at night. I never forget that it is because of them that I am privileged to be a successful writer. I owe my career, my livelihood, and my loyalty to them.

I write books for my readers. As long as they continue to read my novels I really don't mind if the world at large ridicules my work or dismisses it as "trash."

I am satisfied as long as that tired factory worker or that worried mother or that elderly woman in a nursing home finds something, anything, in one of my books that makes her life just a little easier or a little happier.

If my work needs a defense, let that be it.

DIANA PALMER (SUSAN KYLE, DIANA BLAYNE)

Susan Kyle has written sixty-eight series romance novels and eight single title releases (both contemporary and historical) under her own name and under the pen names Diana Palmer and Diana Blayne. Her publishers include Dell, Silhouette, Warner, and Ballantine. There are over six million copies of her books in print.

Her books, including the recent Ballantine release *Lacy*, consistently place in the top ten on the Waldenbooks Romance and Mass Market bestseller lists. She has received five national bestseller awards from Waldenbooks including one for *Reluctant Father*. Her numerous other awards include the Reviewers Choice for Special Achievement Series Romance Storyteller from *Romantic Times* magazine.

Before pursuing her writing career full time, she worked as a reporter on both daily and weekly newspaper staffs.

KATHLEEN GILLES SEIDEL

Judge Me by the Joy I Bring

I can't read Danielle Steele.

This has perplexed me. Several million American women like her work. Why don't I? I can't draw myself up and sigh with smug superiority that she doesn't write well enough. I, believe me, am no snob. It is, I now understand, what Danielle Steele chooses to write about. Her characters are ambitious television journalists and glamorous cardiac surgeons. Being married to a cardiac surgeon is not my idea of glamour; it is my idea of hell.

But if there were a book with a plot similar to Steele's, with the same depth of characterization, the same felicity of expression, and if all those doctors were dukes or if it were set in a small town with the hero something of an outsider, then I might have a thunderingly good time. These are my fantasies, not doctors. I cannot read Danielle Steele because she is not writing about my fantasies.

I assert that fantasy is the most important element in the appeal of popular fiction. I'm not talking only about texts populated by dragons, scorceresses, and vampires. My idea of fantasy is much broader than that, and I focus my definition not on the text but on the reader, the writer, and their experiences.

In a fantasy you are longing, wishing, desiring to walk—for some time at least and perhaps only in the imagination—in some other pair of shoes. A book of popular fiction succeeds when you have, within the reading experience, achieved that desire, when you have singlehandedly saved the wagon train, when you have put on a lilac silk gown with ivory lace around the hem and sleeves. Pleasure and satisfaction result.

Fantasy is not the "shock of recognition" one feels when one's own life or feelings are astonishingly paralleled by a book. Nor is it the relief I felt when reading Diane Chamberlain's *Secret Lives,* in which a young girl's mentally disturbed mother, on learning that her daughter had started menstruating, cut the girl's hair down to her scalp.[1] Whatever my limits as a parent, I *know* that I'm not that bad. That's not a fantasy. I do not need to *wish* to be better than that mother; I *am.*

Fantasy is not something cheap or dirty, a guilty pleasure belonging only to popular fiction. Fantasy can be part of the appeal in other kinds of literature. In high school, I read Sophocles's *Antigone,* a classical Greek tragedy, and I longed to have Antigone's nobility, her commitment to principle. That was a fantasy. Conversely, popular fiction has additional appeals besides fantasy—interesting explications of characters' motivations, suspenseful plots, or comments on the way we live now. But its primary appeal, just as the primary response to tragedy is Aristotle's pity and fear, has to do with fantasy.

This appeal is not at odds with emotional depth or intellectual complexity; one should not think of fantasy as necessarily thin and feebleminded. The richer the fantasy and the more depth and complexity that it has, the immeasurably more satisfying its realization will be. This is true of all popular fiction; I understand its workings best in romance novels.

Fantasy is the power that drives the reading and writing of romances. It is the energy, the magic, the content. Fantasies permeate the books. Critics often refer to a single romance fantasy, but the fantasies are everywhere in the books: in the plot, the character, and the setting.

The plot of a romance novel—especially its happy ending—sets up fantasies about the way the world ought to work. A happy ending is necessary, inevitable. The heroine is guaranteed a husband, a home, and financial security.

Because of the ending's guarantee, the heroine has license to behave, during the unfolding of the plot, in ways that most of us don't dare. She can get angry with the hero and can vent her anger on him. She can reject him; he will always return. She can put herself in the path of physical danger, and if she does have to confront—as many historical heroines do—poverty or violence, she survives without emotional degradation.

The world, of course, does not operate this way. Go jogging at night in Central Park and you might end up brain damaged. Romance readers know this. But when they pick up a romance they are choosing *not* to read about life's darkest possibilities.

I do explore some of my own anxieties as I write my books, but the anxieties are never my deepest. I would, for example, never put a heroine in a situation where her children are suffering and she can do nothing for them. That is my own private horror. I don't want to write about it, and my readers don't come to my books wanting to read about it. There are books that do allow, even encourage, readers to confront their gravest fears. When people want that, they turn to those books, not to a romance.

The characters are the primary vehicle conveying a book's fantasies. The other contributors to this volume will, I am sure, have much to say on the characters, so I limit myself to three points: what happens to the hero when he falls in love, why readers like the much maligned dewy-eyed, passive young heroine, and why the heroines look the way they do.

"Man's love is of man's life a thing apart, / 'Tis woman's whole existence," writes Lord Byron. This is, of course, *his* fantasy. I am a woman, but love is not my whole existence, not unless you include my children and my work, my parents, my friends, the smell of tomato plants, and the window treatments in my living room, all of which I love. I don't think that this is what Byron had in mind.

Nor will the romance novel allow the first half of Byron's sentence to stand. Man's love, says the fantasy of the romance novel, becomes as important to him as it is to the woman. The hero can be—to steal Nora Roberts's phrase—the richest man in the free world, but the heroine and his love for her overwhelm him. At the beginning of the book he may seem cold and self-contained, he may be mysterious and ruthlessly independent. By the end he is deeply in love and thoroughly comprehensible. He thinks about the heroine all the time; she has enormous psychological power over him.

A lot of women don't feel like they have much power, and some romances do have conventional power fantasies in which the heroine has money and clout. But in every romance I can think of, the heroine has the power to stop the hero's emotional traffic, to swirl his attention around her, to place herself in the center of his stage. The more distant he is at the book's opening, the more her power is demonstrated.

"Think you," continues Byron, "if Laura had been Petrarch's wife, / He would have written sonnets all his life?" Yes. Yes, he would—at least if he were the hero of a romance novel.

Janice Radway, in her provocative study of romance readers, *Reading the Romance,* asserts that most women spend much of their time taking care of other people.[2] No one takes care of Mom, except when Mom decides to take care of herself by reading a romance and becoming, for that time, a countess. The richest man in the free world worries about her well-being, he is tender toward her, he is nurturing, and the promise of the ending is that he will do this for the rest of his life. He will write sonnets until he dies.

Romance writers often find themselves doing odd things. I was once asked to judge a Valentine's Day contest sponsored by a local department store. Entrants wrote an essay describing their most romantic moment, and I was to decide which was the most romantic. To do so, I had to think about what makes a moment romantic. What does our culture label romantic? All the entries involved, first, food and drink and, second, an element of surprise. The food and drink were always provided by the other person. As was explicit in the winning entry, these provisions became a symbol of being taken care of, of being a child again.

Childhood, of course, involves more than being taken care of. We remember being little Wordsworthian creatures, absorbed in the immediate, fully engrossed, charged with wonder and joy. The surprise—the second feature of the romantic moment—returns you to that state; it knocks the adult self-consciousness out of you. You can savor and relish a sensual, emotional world. The surprise awakens you into seeing life fresh and anew; the nurturing makes the surprise safe. This is what makes romance heroes romantic. They do both. They surprise you, they unsettle you, they bring drama and excitement, but in the end they make you feel safe.[3]

This fantasy about a return to childhood is nowhere clearer than in the books—written far less frequently than they once were—in which the heroine is quite young. She is pretty, but someone else in the book is staggeringly beautiful. She is kind, but she doesn't have the experience to know what to do with her generous impulses. She is shy, she seems to have no goals, but the hero is desperately in love with her. One critic describes such heroines as being like babies; they are loved just because they are there.[4]

Such books are often harshly judged, but their appeal makes sense to me. In this fantasy, you don't have to earn love. There are brighter people in the world, prettier, more glamorous people, but you are the one who is loved. And you don't have to do a thing to be worthy of it. If you're a woman with a difficult life, if you're struggling to keep up in a competitive corporation, it might be pleasant to spend a few hours feeling as if you aren't always being judged and graded. If you're supporting your children by yourself, if you're having to make all those decisions about their curfews and their schoolwork and their friends on your own, a father figure swooping in to take all that off your shoulders is a pretty thought.

And nothing for anyone to get upset over. This is all taking place in the realm of fantasies. We should not assume that fantasies are necessarily goals, things people actually want. Enjoying such a book doesn't mean you want to sacrifice the sense of accomplishment that comes from success or that you want to abandon your independence and authority for the sake of some over-bearing, overcontrolling male. It only means that your imagination wants to dance, for a moment, a different waltz.

Almost all romance heroines are labeled as physically attractive. Some are called stunningly lovely, others simply pretty and healthy. In most cases, I assert, this isn't much more than a label.

It is a rare romance that really explores the question of what it is like to be beautiful. In real life, people respond to loveliness in complex ways. Some become conciliatory and fawning; others become defensive. This doesn't happen in a romance. The hero admires the heroine's appearance in a fairly straightforward, sexual way, and other characters don't seem affected by it much at all. After the initial description, the heroine's beauty is rarely mentioned except in the sex scenes.

The fantasy, I believe, is not to be beautiful but to have an identity for yourself that is not caught up in your appearance. Romance heroines rarely know how beautiful they really are. This isn't because they are too stupid to look in a mirror or too low in self-esteem to understand what they see there, but because they are presenting the fantasy of being something other than body, of not having any of this cosmetic-advertisement stuff matter.

My editors at Harlequin used to joke that they could always tell when a man had written a manuscript. Somewhere in the first fifty pages the heroine undressed in front of a mirror . . . and liked what she saw. That sounds like a good idea, having a body that you can admire when you are buck-naked in your own bathroom. But what clearly seems a better idea, a more appealing fantasy, is to walk by that mirror and *simply not care.*

One heroine in romance literature who knows exactly what she looks like—and she is the homeliest of them all—is Jenny Chawleigh of Georgette Heyer's *A Civil Contract.* She's "already plump, and would probably become stout in later life."[5] What makes her such an appealing heroine is that she utterly accepts her appearance. She chuckles at how dreadful she will look in her Court dress. She knows that she has many other abilities and—this is crucial—*values herself for them.* She and the physical accident of her short neck and mouse-colored hair don't have much to do with one another.

This fantasy is not limited to the romance genre. Sue Grafton, Sara Paretsky, and the other creators of the hard-boiled female detectives are also presenting heroines without much anxiety about their physical appearances. The first time we meet Kinsey Milhone in Sue Grafton's *"A" Is for Alibi,*[6] she has no appearance. She has a body—she runs and has sex—but she doesn't look like anything. We don't know what color her hair or eyes are; we don't know if she is tall or short, muscular or ethereal. People don't seem to react one way or another to her appearance. Her wardrobe is described only in the most general terms. She notices the clothes and appearance of other female characters, but of her own we hear nothing. In later books she does acquire short, dark hair and that go-everywhere black dress, but these details come without any emotional weight.

The mystery writers probably are conveying the fantasy more directly than we are. To keep the heroine's appearance from being a source of stress we make her beautiful (which is not necessarily a stress-free condition in life). We give her an "A" and pretend that the grade card doesn't exist. The mystery writers don't give out grades at all.

They are perhaps being more honest than we, but they are working in a first person masculine tradition. The appearance and wardrobe of the male hard-boiled detective don't matter to him or to the people he encounters. Mystery readers don't expect much description of hair styles and sleeve length.

Romance readers do. They are interested in the physical detail of the fantasy world. They want to know what the characters look like; they want clothes and rooms described.

Critics often ridicule as trivial this attention to detail in romances, particularly in regard to setting, but, as in any work of fiction, a carefully presented setting helps the reader suspend disbelief. Moreover, in a romance the setting itself may be part of the fantasy.

The first function of the setting of a romance novel is to be Other, to transport the reader to somewhere else. The setting often provides a reader with the first and clearest signal that fantasy follows. When a novel opens "England, 1802. It was only a matter of time before the wedding guests killed one another"; when the next sentence mentions a baron, a king, and a castle; you can be pretty sure that Julie Garwood isn't going to make you drive the soccer carpool, stopping at the Safeway for a gallon of milk and two loaves of whole-wheat bread.[7]

The settings of romance are important for more than just their Other-ness. Particular settings are associated with particular fantasies. The publishers know this. In the first few years of the Harlequin American Romance line, the editor writing the cover copy had only a hundred words in which to describe each book, but she always used some of those words to describe the setting. The covers were dominated by the usual clinch, but a subsidiary element in the artwork always alluded to the setting. Indeed, the first person I ever saw buy one of my books said she was initially intrigued by the little camping tent in the corner of the cover, a detail about the setting.

I find myself surprisingly rigid about what settings I choose to read about. Without an enthusiastic recommendation, I won't read what booksellers call "sand" books, romances with sheiks or oil-rich princes. I will only read about New York City if Beverly Sommers wrote the book. Other readers want nothing to do with medieval times, World War II, or any country between the Tropic of Cancer and the Tropic of Capricorn. Readers are not expressing a preference for kinds of vegetation and climatic conditions. They are responding to the fact that certain fantasies are usually associated with certain times and places.

Frontier romances are full of fantasies about resourcefulness and daring. Regencies tell of a polite, ordered society in which gunfights are elegantly staged duels governed by an elaborate code. Civil War books are charged with private gallantry in the face of public hopelessness. Such books will not necessarily appeal to the same readers. Among the contemporary novels, books set in Los Angeles, New York, and Paris are often "glitz and glamour" stories with wealthy, high-strung characters involved in dramatic confrontations. Books set in small towns tend to be more family oriented.

They are quieter books; emotion builds more slowly and is sustained for longer periods.

Historical romances are more likely to depict poverty, violence, and rape than are romances set in the present.[8] The reason is simple. The historical setting makes the dramatization of such perils more remote and therefore less threatening. Waiting in a welfare line isn't a fantasy that many romance readers would care to participate in. Stealing a pair of breeches and hiring yourself on as a stableboy to an earl who will fall in love with you the instant he knows you are female is a far more engaging way to confront your fears about poverty.

I am overgeneralizing, of course. I can think of an exception to every single type of book I have mentioned in the last two paragraphs. Still, when readers learn that a book has a particular setting, they expect certain kinds of fantasies will follow.

The notion that the romance reader will indiscriminately swallow anything that the publishers dump on her plate is believed only by people who never speak to readers. Individual readers have their own tastes. They make their choices consciously. They are in control of their own reading.

For me, setting makes clearest the difference between fantasies and goals. I write about, fantasize about, small towns because I grew up in a small town and I am fascinated by them, but I no longer want to live in one. The book I enjoyed writing the least was set the closest to my current home, although I love where I live. This book and its ordinary suburban setting raise some interesting questions.[9] My own lesser pleasure in it was mirrored in the response of the readers. Although its sales figures were consistent with those of my previous books, I got the least fan mail on that one. When I speak to readers, it is the one book they never mention. Fewer of its publisher's foreign subsidiaries chose to translate it than have translated my other books.

I do not blame this reaction entirely on the book's setting, but that setting—as does the setting in every romance—reflects the nature of the fantasies, and of all my books, the appeal of fantasy is the least in this one. There is some socioeconomic detail about the upper middle class that might attract some readers, but it is mostly a portrait of two people putting their marriage back together step by step. Although I was not entirely aware of it at the time, my notion of my reader was not someone who was fantasizing about the situation but someone who was, in her own life, going through something similar. Unconsciously I chose a setting that mirrored this closer connection to a real-life referent. There is, of course, nothing in the world wrong with a novelist writing to such a reader, but a series romance is not the best place to do it. When a reader chooses to pick up a romance as opposed to another kind of book, she is expecting a certain kind of reading experience. In that book, I offered a different kind. No one suggested that I be stoned, but no one thanked me for it either.

What then is the significance of fantasy's being so central to the experience of popular fiction?

To start with, an author's fantasies determine how successful he or she will be in the popular fiction market. There are two issues involved.[10]

First, your success will depend on how many people share your fantasies. If your most cherished daydream involves killing people with your bare hands, you are not going to do very well in the romance market. Not many romance readers have those fantasies. If, however, you dream about being on the run with a half-naked fellow named Grey Eagle, you may do all right.

I believe—and this is a very Romantic view of romance writing—that you are more or less doomed to write certain kinds of books. You can only write your own fantasies. A friend of mine spent two years trying to write short, sexy contemporaries because such books made more money than did the Regencies she loved. Not one of them sold. Then she wrote a Regency, which resulted almost immediately in a multi-book contract. She makes less per book than a contemporary author, but she can write Regencies with grace, joy, and success, and she couldn't write contemporaries at all.

At the moment, more historical authors are reaching the bestseller lists than are writers of contemporary romances. I would like to be on more bestseller lists. So why don't I rush out and write a historical?

Because it wouldn't work. Absolute sincerity about your fantasies is like yeast. If there is none in the kitchen, forget about making a recipe that calls for it. It is the one thing for which there are no substitutions. There have been plenty of competent, professional writers over the last ten years who have thought to make a quick buck by writing a romance. They claim that all they'll need to do is figure out the formula. They count the number of pages between kisses, write their book, and then write articles about how surprised they are that the book was rejected.

Literary competence does help. However many people share an author's fantasies, the second thing that determines her success is how well she conveys those fantasies. Some of us are simply better at it than others.

No one talks about this very much. Some scholars

who write on the romance seem unable to distinguish one book from another. As an author, this irritates me no end. How can a person talk about the books when she is not paying enough attention to distinguish our individual voices?

Other critics are better readers. Kay Mussell is alert and sensitive; she knows when an author is doing something that hasn't been done before.[11] But in her discussion of individual books she focuses almost entirely on content and vision as a way of discriminating among them. It is a valid approach, but one that avoids, by design I assume, all the usual ways one evaluates a book.

Similarly, when Janice Radway explicates a bookseller's five-star rating system, she looks for how the ratings reflect the book's political content. Books receiving only one star fail because "they ask the reader to identify with a heroine who is hurt, humiliated, and brutalized."[12] I realize that Radway is not writing conventional literary criticism, but to be unwilling to say that one-star romances fail because they are badly executed implies that good execution is not important to romance readers, and that, I think, is wrong and unfair.

But what do we mean by good execution? Why are the good romances good? And what is bad about the bad ones? (When judged by conventional textual standards, many very successful, very cherished romance novels do seem weak.)

One element is the power of fantasy. Fantasies enthrall and fascinate. If a reader's fantasies and a writer's fantasies are very similar, the reader will so want to be wearing that doeskin robe or riding in that well-sprung chaise over cobbled roads that the writer's job of putting her there is not a difficult one.

But there is still the question of qualitative differences among the books. Some are more powerful than others. Everyone knows that; no one does a very good job of talking about it.

We may not have a vocabulary with which to evaluate a text for the qualities that make fantasies vivid and immediate. The usual categories about tightly constructed plots and consistent, believable characters may not be relevant. The books have strengths that no one knows how to describe. Can anyone locate in a text exactly which words make a fantasy come alive? How can we account for the power of these books?[13]

"How do you make the characters' emotions feel so real?" unpublished authors ask me. "How do you make me cry?" I have a Ph.D. in the theory of the novel. I have written—counting the ones in a drawer—eleven of the creatures, but I can't answer that question. I don't know. I can talk about plot structure, pacing, point of view, and character development, all the things studied in the classroom. But my own particular strength, using printed words to get someone to feel like someone else, feeling something else, that ability which has made me a novelist—I have no words to tell you how I can do that.

In the last eight to ten years, romance novels have been extremely responsive to the social issues raised by mainstream feminism. We have changed the notion of what heroines can be and what they can do. They can be older. They can be sexually experienced. Some are divorced; some are mothers. We have put them in traditionally masculine jobs. They build bridges, finance shopping malls, and found ice cream empires. The historical heroines take over their father's medical practice, run the family newspaper, or put on their brother's breeches and ride out to battle. Many heroines plan to keep working after their marriages. At the end of Susan Elizabeth Phillips's *Hot Shot,* the now happily-married heroine announces that this is her company, and she is going to turn the executive dining room into an on-site day care center[14] (something which incidentally the Toronto office of Harlequin does have; that company stays in business by knowing what women want).

Actually, in the mid-1980s there was considerable editorial pressure on writers to conform to at least the appearance of a more feminist fantasy. I had a dying woman say to her college-aged son, "You'll want this jewelry for the girl you marry." An editor changed "girl" to "young woman." "Girl," she told me, was a word never to be used for a female over eighteen. I put it back in. While I now cringe at my excessive use of the word "girl" in my overly conventional first book, I am not going to have a character speak out of voice so that my editors and I will appear to have better political credentials.

My problems were minor. During this time, some writers were extremely unhappy, wearied by struggles with young, politically conscious editors. The authors felt that an alien sensibility was being forced on their work, that they weren't being allowed to speak to their readers in their own voices. They didn't want to write about heroines who repair helicopters. The authors who were drawn to the macho, domineering hero had similar difficulties. One such author has said that she has never had an editor who has truly been in sympathy with her work. Her sales figures—that is, the readers—have allowed her to be true to her own vision. Ironically, often the authors who are the most popular with readers have gotten the most pressure to change their fantasies.

Things are calmer now. Romance editing ages a girl fast. Those young editors either have quit or are several decades older than they were ten years ago.

But as we pride ourselves on giving our heroines professions, on making them more sexually aggressive, I wonder if we have really addressed the feminists' more interesting challenges. In the remaining section of this essay, I would like to address three such topics—that romance writers are not helping women to change their lives, that the books are over-consoling, and that the books are addictive.

Many feminists look at women's lives today and see much that ought to be changed. They fault romances for not promoting such change. "In the end," Radway writes in her conclusion, "the romance-reading process gives the reader a strategy for making her present situation more comfortable without a substantive reordering of its structure rather than a comprehensive program for reorganizing her life in such a way that all needs might be met."[15]

A comprehensive program for reorganizing her life? Who on earth am I that I should be telling another woman how to reorganize her life?

One answer is that at least I am someone who feels close to romance readers. The feminists, I am afraid, do not. Janice Radway flew out to the Midwest feeling some trepidation about her scheduled meeting with a romance bookseller who had promised to identify herself by wearing a lavender pantsuit.[16] As I interpret Radway's engaging account of the meeting, she is astonished at how readily she liked the bookseller, a warm, magnanimous, open-hearted woman.

Well of course, you liked her, I say to my copy of *Reading the Romance*. Romance booksellers are likable people. You don't have to have the same fashion sense—or have the same education or come from the same socioeconomic class—to like a person. With our interest in the personal, romance writers often transcend the barriers that separate others. I have a long and expensive education behind me. Some of my readers do too; others do not. My closest friend in the romance community is a high school graduate. We are all women; we can talk to one another.

Feminists talk about sisterhood; I do not know how deeply they feel it. The undercurrent throughout feminist criticism of romances is that these scholars and critics know what is right for other women—and oh my, do they feel the "us/them" distinction acutely. In a doctoral dissertation of which I have unfortunately seen only the introduction and the first chapter, Deborah K. Chappel carefully traces the scholarly studies of romances and finds in all the work, however sympathetic the authors hope to be, a strong sense of the reader as Other, as someone less enlightened, less analytic—more likely to wear a lavender pantsuit—than the critic.[17] They, those scholars, aren't like you and me, and they're mighty glad of it. Nonetheless, they know what you and I should be doing with our lives.

I stray from the subject. I have not answered the challenge—that I, as a romance writer, am not helping readers to change their lives. My answer is simple— that's right, I'm not.

Let us suppose for a moment that I know how to help men develop the nurturing qualities that society has repressed in them—something Radway regrets that romances offer no instruction upon.[18] If I were possessed of such information, is a romance novel the best place for me to impart it to the world?

These are not self-help books. They are fantasies. They are entertainment. They are pleasure. My reader comes to my book when she is tired. Reading my book is the one thing, often the only thing, that she is doing for herself that day, that week. Reading may be the only way she knows how to relax. If I am able to give her a few delicious, relaxing hours, that is a noble enough purpose for me.

I do have beliefs about the way people ought to live, and naturally these find their way into my work. But these thoughts are not the most important thing happening. All the practical advice in my putting-your-marriage-back-together book, which was my least popular, could probably be presented in a five-page essay. If romance reading has encouraged some women to improve their lives, if it has made them more independent, if it has increased their sense of their own value, that is grand. But such real-life change is not, I think, the standard by which we should judge our work. (I even wonder how well self-help books would fare if rigorously scrutinized by that standard.) Judge me on the joy I bring.

I do not feel a responsibility to tell readers how to live their lives. Romances are not the only influences women encounter. I read Emilie Loring in junior high, Georgette Heyer in high school, and Harlequin Presents in graduate school. But with all due respect to those authors it is from my mother that I got my sense of what a woman can do with her life. She got her M.D. at 22; she practiced medicine part-time so that she could lead Girl Scout troops and teach Sunday school. Not surprisingly, both my sister and I are married mothers who work part-time in jobs we adore. Attesting even more vividly to the power of role models in shaping women's lives is that, of the nine gir—young women—

in my mother's Senior Scout troop, two of them and the younger sister of one of those are now physicians, two of the three having chosen my mother's specialty.

Yes, people get information about life from their reading, but they test that against other data. Too often when I read feminist commentary on romance readers, the picture that emerges is of children with childish reading strategies. Romance readers are grown women, able to distinguish between art and life, the literary and the actual.

Such assumptions about the childishness of romance readers were at the heart of the birth-control-in-the-sex-scenes struggle several years ago. "It is irresponsible not to mention birth control," some editors announced. No, many of us answered, it may be irresponsible not to *practice* birth control, but *mentioning* it in a work of fantasy read by adults is not a necessary duty. My readers know where babies come from.

Of course, by not being part of the solution—by not showing readers how to reorganize their lives—we are, some critics continue, part of the problem. This is the second feminist criticism I shall address, that romances aren't simply something nice a tired woman does for herself, that they numb her, sedate her, overconsole her. Radway finds it "tempting to suggest that romantic fiction must be an active agent in the maintenance of the ideological status quo because it ultimately reconciles women to partriarchal society and reintegrates them with its institutions."[19] Other feminists raise the question, too. Romance writers, they say, are persuading women to endure what ought to be unendurable. We are muting the call to arms.

This is, on some levels, impossible to answer for it is impossible to prove. As Radway admits, none of us know what romance readers would be doing if they did not have romances to read.

My response then is to the major premise, and I think at this level lies the most profound disagreement between the feminists writing about romances and the novelists writing the books themselves. It is possible to locate similarities—that we both move women and their concerns to the center of the picture—but the fundamental vision of women's lives differs. I don't think things are all that bad.

Kay Mussell writes that romance reading provides "an *escape from* powerlessness, *from* meaninglessness, and *from* lack of self-esteem and identity"[20] (Mussell's emphasis). I am a romance reader, and I strongly object to anyone describing my life in those terms. I have my moments of dissatisfaction, of course, but I have power and meaning, I do not lack self-esteem or identity.

Granted not all women have living room window treatments that they like as much as I like mine, or a mother such as mine or work that they feel about as I feel about mine, but I do think it is possible for women to find contentment, fulfillment, peace, and happiness within our culture, and I believe that a great many of them are doing a good job of it.

There is, of course, an easy response to my affirmation. I am trapped in "false consciousness," I am so oppressed that I don't know that I am oppressed. I only *think* I am happy. If I knew what they know, I would know that I wasn't. This is, of course, unanswerable—as it was designed to be. It turns me into a child, without any insight into my own condition.

And not only are we children, we are addicts. Tania Modleski compares romances to tranquilizers. "The user must constantly increase the dosage of the drug in order to alleviate problems aggravated by the drug itself."[21] I would point out that she offers no evidence at all to support this comparison.

Repetitive reading—people rereading the same books or reading books that are similar to ones they have already read—is a phenomenon that does concern the feminists. I will not accept the "addict" label, but I certainly plead guilty to repetitive reading. When I was in graduate school I would occasionally take the day off and read five or six Harlequin Presents. When I was twelve, my parents gave me a paperback of *Gone with the Wind* for Christmas. I read it seven times that year. The next year Santa brought it to me in hardcover. There continue to be books I reread regularly.

Kay Mussell and Tania Modleski, feminist scholars, blame repetitive reading on the ending of the book. The fantasy of the happy ending, they assert, is precarious, even false, as it is based on "the failure of a patriarchy to imagine a wider vision of women's lives"[22] and "the insistent denial of the reality of male hostility towards women."[23] The ending, although it provides temporary relief,[24] is thus inherently unsatisfying, "so unsatisfying that the story must be told over and over."[25] "Readers must constantly return to the same text (to texts which are virtually the same) in order to be reconvinced."[26] The endings have so little to do with life that they are believable only fleetingly, and the desperate reader must seize another book to try to recapture that brief—and false—pleasure.

I don't dispute the authenticity of Mussell's and Modleski's reading experience; the pleasure they feel at the endings of the books may well be undercut by a profound political uneasiness. I don't feel that way. In a well-done book, the happy ending becomes for me a satisfying, convincing, imaginatively realized fantasy. And I don't think that the habit of repeated readings necessarily proves that hundreds of thousands of American women read like them, not me.

Their argument, by focusing only on the political message of the ending, ignores the fact that the pleasures of fantasies pervade the book. It is fun to read, early in Georgette Heyer's *The Devil's Cub,* the Marquis of Vidal's cool resolve to race his curricle to Newmarket immediately after fighting a duel. It is even more fun to follow the restrained, ironic language in which his ducal father afterwards banishes him to the Continent.[27] Romances are full of delicious moments, some funny, some heartwarming, some sensually evocative. That's why I reread *The Devil's Cub* every few years. I am not desperately seeking out the ending so that it will assure me that it is possible to be happy within our patriarchal culture's institutions. I am relishing the book's entire experience with the ongoing accumulation of fantasy's pleasures, small and large.

If we must have a critical apparatus in which to discuss repetitive reading, I think that information theory might be more useful than politics. One reason, for example, that I reread books is that I read so quickly the first time that subsequent rereadings provide new information. Or I might reread a book I know very well because at that moment I am so very tired that I do not want one single scrap of new information.

We ought not to forget that reading romances is not the only thing human beings do repetitively. Most leisure activities are compelling. It's hard to stand up from a jigsaw puzzle. My mother doesn't like to sew at night because she knows it will be hard to quit. I have neighbors who might be candidates for a twelve-step program for compulsive gardeners. My husband has trouble turning off a baseball game—the next batter might turn the game around—and he watches hundreds (at least it seems like hundreds) every summer.

Yes, there are some women who have allowed reading to take over their lives. Occasionally you do meet someone at an autographing who leaves you heartsick, but let us not generalize too quickly from this occasional instance. Not every woman with a chocolate chip cookie in hand has an eating disorder.

I am tired of the assumption that reading romances proves that there is something wrong with a woman's life. She ought to change her life, the thinking goes, so that whatever needs are met by her books will be met by her life.

But books are a part of life. They are a source of splendid pleasure. No one can expect to have all his or her emotional needs met by a single source, whether mate, children, friends, professional pursuits, or leisure activities. It is tragic when a woman has nothing in her life except books, but it is, I think, equally tragic when a man has only his job.

Life is a complex business with needs that vary by the moment. For many women, romances are a part of a very complicated equation that makes their lives work. At a family holiday several years ago, my sister's three sons were all under the age of seven and all had intestinal flu, and my sister, a person I treasure, wasn't feeling so great herself. My mother and I took over the boys and banished her to bed with my latest manuscript for company. An hour later, I looked in on her. She was sitting in bed, and in the middle of this vexing, exhausting day *she was smiling*.

Of course, under these circumstances, simply being

off-duty, simply being by herself, would have been a relief. But to be by yourself *and* have a good book to read—the relief becomes joy.

So to my readers I say—I'm not going to come take care of your kids when they are sick, but when you have a moment away from them or from the latest project at work or from whatever are the stresses in your life, my book will be there for you. I shall do all that I can to write one that is worthy of the precious time you give it. I do this because you too are my sister.

NOTES

1. Diane Chamberlain, *Secret Lives* (New York: HarperCollins, 1991), 27.

2. Janice Radway, *Reading the Romance: Women, Patriarchy, and Popular Literature* (Chapel Hill: University of North Carolina Press, 1984), 94. In this article I disagree often with Radway. I think, for example, that by speaking only to women who were known to their bookseller she gravely limited her sense of who the readers are. But I must underscore that my most positive sense of myself as a romance writer emerged from her book. Her idea that romance reading is the one thing that many women do for themselves has sanctified my work for me.

3. Which aspect of the hero is emphasized the most determines whether he is an "alpha male" or a "wimp." What interests me about this distinction is that, so far as I know, this is the only piece of jargon that has originated from the authors themselves, even though we are a close-knit community with astonishing lines of communication.

I view this lack of jargon as evidence of two things.

First is the absolute sincerity with which we view our books. Glib, dismissive jargon does not feel appropriate. Second is that we view each book as unique. What matters to us is how each book differs from the others, something that jargon does not account for.

The term "alpha male" came into use, I believe, because some authors were engaged in a struggle with editors about a certain type of hero and needed a vocabulary for the discussion.

4. Ann Douglas, "Soft-Porn Culture," *New Republic* (30 August 1980): 25–29.

5. Georgette Heyer, *A Civil Contract* (New York: Ace Books, 1961), 57.

6. Sue Grafton, *"A" is for Alibi* (New York: Holt, Rinehart, and Winston, 1982).

7. Julie Garwood, *The Gift* (New York: Pocket Books, 1991), 1. I do not mean to suggest that driving a soccer carpool cannot be a fantasy. When I was in the depths of infertility treatment, it was, believe me, one of mine.

8. The literature on the rape fantasy is considerable. Explanations for the fantasy vary: women have been conditioned to be victims; women want to control and confront their fears imaginatively; women do not want to accept responsibility for sexual desire; and so on. Helen Hazen in *Endless Rapture: Rape, Romance, and the Female Imagination* (New York: Charles Scribner's Sons, 1983) defends the rape fantasy with many interesting insights, although she does accuse feminists who repudiate the fantasy of denying and repressing their own fantasies. I found that accusation offensive.

9. *When Love Isn't Enough,* Harlequin American Romance #80 (Toronto: Harlequin Books, 1984).

10. I am ignoring the publisher's role in one's suc-

cess—the quality of the cover art and copy, the book's position on the list, the amount of advertising, and so forth. This is unquestionably important.

11. Kay Mussell, *Fantasy and Reconciliation: Contemporary Formulas of Women's Romantic Fiction* (Westport, CT: Greenwood Press, 1984).

12. Radway, 178.

13. Melinda Helfer reviews contemporaries and Regencies for *Romantic Times* in prose that I often think is better than my own. In reviews of books she admires the most, she usually focuses on the emotional response the book produces. When she likes a book less well, then she turns to more conventional terminology: "predictable plot," "overly familiar characters," and so on. Her reviews are never more than a few sentences long, but anyone wanting to develop a more sensitive critical vocabulary ought, I think, start by talking to her.

14. Susan Elizabeth Phillips, *Hot Shot* (New York: Pocket Books, 1991), 484.

15. Radway, 215.

16. Radway, 57.

17. Deborah K. Chappel, *American Romances: Narratives of Culture and Identity* (Ph.D. dissertation, Duke University, 1991), 78. Chappel's own thesis—that by reading romances women are attempting to see themselves in the best possible light—will be welcomed by romance writers.

Janice Radway, in her 1987 introduction to the British edition of *Reading the Romance,* which I have read only in manuscript form, acknowledges the "residual elitism which assumes that feminist intellectuals alone know what is best for all women." In a graceful, moving statement, she suggests that such scholars should offer romance readers and writers "our support rather than our criticism or direction." She follows this generous-hearted position with the most discouraging words I encountered in all the reading I did for this essay as she dismisses the possibility: "Our segregation by class, occupation, and race [*race?*] works against us." We are still Other to her; she does not believe either party can speak to the other. I find this inexpressibly sad.

18. Radway, 129.

19. Radway, 217.

20. Mussell, 164.

21. Tania Modleski, *Loving with A Vengeance: Mass-Produced Fantasies for Women* (Hamden, CT: Archon Books, 1982), 57.

22. Mussell, 184.

23. Modleski, 111.

24. Mussell, 164.

25. Mussell, 184.

26. Modleski, 111.

27. Georgette Heyer, *The Devil's Cub* (London: Pan Books, 1932/1969), 62, 77–80.

KATHLEEN GILLES SEIDEL

Kathleen Gilles Seidel is the author of nine contemporary romance novels. Her first was one of the launch titles for the Harlequin American Romance line, and her next five books were written for Harlequin. She now writes for Pocket Books. Her recent releases include *Maybe This Time* and *More Than You Dreamed*.

Her books have won numerous awards, including the Romance Writers of America Golden Medallion Award. She has a Ph.D. in English literature from the Johns Hopkins University and participated in the School for Criticism and Theory sponsored by the National Endowment for the Humanities. Of all her professional accomplishments and recognition, nothing means more to her than that Harlequin book club subscribers voted her 1984 book *After All These Years* as their favorite Harlequin romance.

Bibliography

Bradley, Marion Zimmer. "Introduction." In Bradley, ed., *Sword and Sorceress VI: An Anthology of Heroic Fantasy.* New York: DAW Books, 1990.

Chappel, Deborah K. *American Romances: Narratives of Culture and Identity.* Ph.D. dissertation, Duke University, 1991.

Douglas, Ann. "Soft-Porn Culture." *New Republic* (20 August 1980): 25–29.

Hazen, Helen. *Endless Rapture: Rape, Romance, and the Female Imagination.* New York: Charles Scribner's Sons, 1983.

Krentz, Jayne Ann. "The Alpha Male." *Romance Writers Report* 10, 1 (1990): 26–28.

Macro, Lucia. "Heroes for Our Time: Silhouette Desire Announces 1989 Is the Year of the Man." *Romance Writers Report* 9, 1 (1989): 43.

Maxwell, Ann and Jayne Ann Krentz. "The Wellsprings of romance." *Romance Writers Report* 9, 5 (1989): 21–23.

Modleski, Tania. *Loving with a Vengeance: Mass Produced Fantasies for Women.* Hamden, CT: Archon Books, 1982.

Mussell, Kay. *Fantasy and Reconciliation: Contemporary Formulas of Women's Romantic Fiction.* Westport, CT: Greenwood Press, 1984.

Radway, Janice. *Reading the Romance: Women, Patriarchy, and Popular Literature.* Chapel Hill: University of North Carolina Press, 1984.

Thurston, Carol. *The Romance Revolution: Erotic Novels for Women and the Quest for a New Sexual Identity.* Urbana: University of Illinois Press, 1987.

Index

JAYNE ANN KRENTZ (Amanda Quick, Jayne Castle, Stephanie James) has written and published more than fifty series romances for several publishers including Harlequin, Silhouette, and Dell. Currently she writes contemporary romances for Pocket Books under her own name and historical romances for Bantam under the pen name Amanda Quick. Several of her contemporary and historical titles, including *Scandal, Rendezvous, Sweet Fortune,* and *Perfect Partners,* appeared on the *New York Times* bestseller list.